STARTING
RIGHT
IN YOUR
NEW
BUSINESS

Wilfred Tetreault, C.B.C., C.B.O.A.
President, American Business Consultants, Inc.

Robert W. Clements, Broker, C.B.O.A.

STARTING RIGHT IN YOUR NEW BUSINESS

Revised Edition

ADDISON-WESLEY PUBLISHING COMPANY

**Reading, Massachusetts • Menlo Park, California • New York
Don Mills, Ontario • Wokingham, England • Amsterdam • Bonn
Sydney • Singapore • Tokyo • Madrid • San Juan**

Library of Congress Cataloging-in-Publication Data

Tetreault, Wilfred F., 1927–
  Starting right in your new business.

  1. Small business—Purchasing. 2. Business enter-
prises, Sale of. I. Clements, Robert W. II. Title.
HD62.7.T47 1988   658.1'141   87-19464
ISBN 0-201-07795-7

ISBN 0-201-07795-7
  BCDEFGH-DO-898

Second Printing, August 1988

Contents

Introduction

Ownership of your own business—"The American Dream"—is an overwhelming drive for millions of American and foreign investors. Many people feel the need to escape the eight-to-five syndrome, nonidentity in the corporate maze, and the stagnation of bureaucracy.

Two and a half million businesses change hands every year, and six hundred thousand new ones start up. The seventeen million or so businesses in operation in the United States today cover a wide spectrum—from the "Mom and Pop" corner store to the large national manufacturing corporations. These businesses offer many opportunities to over twenty-five million investing Americans. There is, at this time, a heavy demand to place buying and selling knowledge in the hands of business owners and buyers.

Every business is for sale at some point in time. However, most business owners do not know how to sell their businesses, and most would-be buyers do not know how to buy businesses! This book, "Starting *Right* in Your New Business," is for the business owner who is contemplating selling a business and the potential buyer who is contemplating buying a business. It is also for the professional CPA, attorney, appraiser, real estate broker or agent, banker, and escrow holder who must understand the buyers' and sellers' needs, wants, ambitions, and so on.

The most important thing to know in starting your first, second, or third business or maintaining an existing business is understanding how to start and operate it right. That means knowing the right questions to ask about the complete business operation: such as financing, appraising, buying, selling, avoiding legal problems, and tax planning and tax savings, not only for the present but for the future as well.

This book will show you which questions to ask, how to avoid mistakes and pitfalls, and how to evaluate your own personal assets and skills objectively. Time spent now studying the feasibility of operation and finance for a potential venture will pay good dividends in the long run.

While investigating buying and selling a business, keep in the back of your mind how you would reconstruct the profit and loss statements if you were buying or selling a business for *cash* and operating it on a *cash* basis. This allows you to usefully compare one business to another.

Study this book with an open, honest, and realistic frame of mind. There are no right or wrong answers. It is a simple matter of evaluating yourself; the decision to buy or sell is up to you. That decision is a very important one; it concerns not only you but also your family and your future.

If you decide to buy or sell a concern, read our book entitled "Buying and Selling Business Opportunities," published by Addison-Wesley in 1981. This book describes and gives examples of appraising forms, listings, agreements, purchase agreements, escrow instructions, form letters, and everything else you will need to complete a sales transaction; and offers a step-by-step checklist as well.

If, after going through that book, you feel you need further instructions, you may attend either of two seminars. One concentrates on the entire bulk sale transfer, and attendees will become "Certified Business Opportunity Appraisers/Consultants." The other seminar covers business opportunity appraising. These seminars are given by the author, Wilfred F. Tetreault, president of American Business Consultants, Inc. (1540 Nuthatch Lane, Sunnyvale, CA 94087), at real estate boards, colleges, universities, and hotels in many cities throughout the United States, and endorsed by the Society of Certified Business Opportunity Appraisers (CBOA), the only national organization of professional business opportunity appraisers with members in fifty states. If you decide to have a professional person assist you in your search for a buyer or seller, ask enough questions before making your final decision.

1

Should I
Buy
My Own Business?

Before we discuss whether or not you should buy your own business, we suggest a brief experiment: Put this book down for a moment, close your eyes, and pick out the single most valuable asset in your ownership of a business.

It's amazing! Whenever we ask this question of people who work for themselves, they invariably pick out a material object. If they are store owners, they point to a new cash register or display case. If they are realtors, they consider the new car most important. To a person who has a photocopy business, the new duplicating machine seems far superior to any other tangible asset. Seldom do they pick out their most important asset: *themselves!*

YOU ARE YOUR MOST IMPORTANT ASSET

The people who pay for your services don't buy just the material product: they buy you—your intelligence, judgment, and skill. In your business *you* are the tangible asset that can make the business you choose to buy a *real* success; *you* are the irreplaceable machine!

Now that you know you are the single most important factor to the success of your business, we want to discuss the rewards and drawbacks of business ownership.

YOU ARE THE BOSS

Because you are "The Boss," your actions are based on independent decisions. Making decisions about aspects of your business—being at the helm of your own ship—is personally rewarding. And, because you are the boss, the work hours are set by you. Consequently, the worry of being fired or the threat of being laid off does not exist. With such typical corporate nightmares removed, the creative drive within you reaches maximum proportions. You will find that your ability to think and act creatively as well as decisively may be the most important force behind the success you are striving for.

Buyers should look at prospective businesses with an eye to their ability to earn a *fair* return on their investment, after deducting a reasonable salary. The earning power and future potential of the business is of prime importance, even though the idea of being the boss may rank higher than the actual income of the business.

As your business grows you will need to hire employees, which will create income leverage for you. An employee-operated business can increase the level of your income: Let others make money for you! The result then of your hard work, creative initiative, and personal decision-making power will be financial reward in terms of profits. Since the level of profits you make directly reflects the level of your initiative and dedication to high standards, you receive an additional reward—social status. Most business owners are held in high regard by the community they serve.

Now that we have pointed out the personal rewards of owning your business—the independence, the chance for creativity, the profits, and the social status which are all the result of personal ability—we must point out some problems which, if left unchecked by you the owner, can ruin an otherwise profitable endeavor. First, since you are independent, "The Boss," 100 percent of the responsibility rests on your shoulders. The actions you take, based on personal decisions, may fail; so you must be prepared to live emotionally as well as financially with the consequences.

Second, although private business does not lock you into an eight-to-five routine, most require more hours each day for survival, growth, and ultimate success. We emphasize, however, that your time is definitely your own. Many people have bought businesses precisely for this reason. They were successful because they discovered that success resulted from the amount of time spent creatively making decisions.

You will take on the management and supervisory demands normally relegated to the "higher-ups" in the traditional corporate structure. This supervision of business and personnel is necessary because, as you must realize, no one cares about your business as much as you do. Often inconvenient and time-consuming, supervision frequently drains the emotions and places demands on family, friends, and your leisure time. The store owner who consistently decides to go shopping, or bowling, or to a bar after closing, instead of cleaning up, ordering materials, and tending to other duties required to make a business successful, could be in serious trouble within a relatively short time.

The demands on your time can also sap the creative drive you need to make innovative and provocative changes in your business image. Consequently, make sure you protect your creative ability. It can easily become buried under the day-to-day operating routine or the strain of financial and personnel crises.

Moreover, income leverage, although a valuable asset, can work against you regardless of the profitability of your business. Your employees require fair salaries and demand raises. Negative leverage can bury you financially. Providing you have a healthy business to start with, your profits will reflect your personal efforts and your relations with employees, suppliers, and community groups. A business that, unknown to you, had been run into the ground prior to your ownership carries a high risk, especially in the area of profit yield. If your business declines because of any of these points, your social status, community image, and recognition as a leader will be jeopardized.

Although your time is your own, there are nevertheless many external demands to be met. Because the business entity interacts with many outside forces, you as the owner will deal with customers, creditors, suppliers, and state and federal tax boards and governing agencies, as well as landlords, accountants, lawyers, and financial systems. All will make demands on a daily basis, draining your "time bank." Time to spend on more creative and productive projects may dwindle if you allow business matters to become unmanageable.

You are the "irreplaceable machine" in your business, and so you are vulnerable to a problem that affects hundreds of thousands of Americans every year: the inability to earn income because of injuries or sickness. If you become disabled for an extended period of time, there would be no employer to help you out. Who would step in and take over? One answer is, of course, family and friends. But for how long could you expect them to carry on successfully in your footsteps? Another alternative is to detail prior to buying the business every possible thing that could go wrong; then work out the terms with the financial institution financing your enterprise to insure against physical disability.

In closing this chapter, we recommend that you evaluate yourself thoroughly and honestly—your skills, your strengths and weaknesses, and your family. You must face reality: Are you comfortable operating a business? Do you have the qualifications, fortitude, and determination to succeed despite the obstacles? This book helps you look more closely at yourself and your circumstances to determine whether or not buying or selling a business is the best thing for you to do.

At this point, therefore, take an honest inventory of the following: your age, personal health, capabilities, skills, lifestyle, hours available, risk, and the effect of all these on your family. Will they support you in this new endeavor? Will they help you meet this new opportunity?

The scoreboard below can help you make a wise choice. If you are honest in your evaluation, you will get a good indication of how suitable you will be as an independent business owner. Rate yourself *honestly* on a scale of 1 (low) to 10 (high) for each question. Keep in mind the type of business you are considering.

SCOREBOARD EVALUATION TEST

Personal/Management

_____ Can you make decisions and take responsibility?
_____ Do you have common business sense?
_____ Do you possess self-discipline?
_____ Can you get things done on time?
_____ Are you creative?
_____ Are you willing to make sacrifices?

_____ Can you work under pressure while still enjoying your work and other people?

_____ Are you willing to work twelve hours a day, six days a week?

_____ Can you take helpful criticism and advice?

_____ Are you honest and ethical with people?

_____ Do you have the personality to deal with people all day?

_____ Are you adaptable? Are you able to change your opinion when necessary?

_____ Are you motivated? Do you have perseverance? Do you have initiative?

_____ Can you supervise and organize yourself and others?

_____ Are your technical skills adaptable?

_____ Can you inspire confidence?

_____ Do you have leadership?

_____ Do you convey sincerity?

_____ Do you have management skills?

_____ Can you initiate and maintain inventory, sales, tax, and other business records?

_____ Are you able to interpret and fill out government and business forms?

_____ Can you negotiate with suppliers and creditors?

_____ Can you work alone?

_____ Can you make your own decisions?

_____ Do you have short- and long-term goals?

_____ Do you tire easily?

_____ Total

Marketing/Promotions

_____ Do you have skills in marketing? in public relations? in display and packaging promotion and advertising?

_____ Do you know your city? its locations? its traffic conditions?

_____ Have you studied your competition and market needs?

_____ Do you know local laws, rules, and regulations?

_____ Do you know your distribution area?

_____ Do you belong to any trade associations?

_____ Have you the ability to design, redecorate, and make a business more attractive within a reasonable budget?

_____ Can you price your goods competitively?

_____ Total

Financial

_____ Can you survive failure? Do you have the ability to pay all you owe?

_____ Have you checked the profit and loss statements of similar businesses? the range of profit for each expense category?

_____ Are you financially able to enter the business world?

_____ Are you able to get advice from accountants or banker friends?

_____ Do you have sufficient income to live on for six months to one year during your start-up period?

_____ Are you willing to make financial sacrifices during your first year in business?

_____ Do you understand business profit and loss statements and accounting methods?

_____ Have you set up a reasonable budget and a business plan?

_____ Do you have a reserve fund?

_____ Total

Now divide the category totals by the number of questions in each section. This will give you an average rating of your abilities. Reevaluate your shortcomings in each category. Can you gain the knowledge or skill necessary to avoid potential problems in these areas? Should you delay your plans to buy your own business until you gain more knowledge or skill? Would you be better off with knowledgeable partners, or selling your own services to others?

2

Choosing a Business

There are three important factors in choosing a business and number 3 is the most important:

1. What type of business is for me?

2. What are my needs?

3. *Location! Location! Location!*

WHAT EXPERIENCE AND SKILLS DO I HAVE?

Study the accompanying table, "What Type of Business Is for Me?," and evaluate your knowledge, rating yourself 1 (low) to 10 (high) by experience and skill for each type of business listed. (In the blank spaces you may list any other types of businesses you prefer to establish.) Read the list of business ideas below before you make up your mind. (Those marked with an *x* usually do well in an inflationary economy.) Once you have rated yourself, add up the totals under *each* business listed and you will see a trend toward the type of business you prefer. Try to get into a business you have always wanted to be in. If you are afraid of failure or of losing your money, continue to work outside your own business at a part-time job for a short time. Most people who fail in business fail because of inexperience and lack of back-up money to help out in emergencies.

Business Suggestions

Advertising Agencies

Ambulance Services

Amusement Centers

Answering Services

Antique Stores

Appliance Repair Stores

Art Schools

x Art Supply Stores

Auctioneers

Auto Dealerships

Auto Parts Stores

Auto Repair Shops

Auto Tire Stores

Auto Washes

Bail Bonds

Bait Shops

Bakeries

Barber Shops

Beauty Shops

Beer Bars

x Bicycle Stores & Repairs

Billiard Parlors

Boat Sales

Bowling Alleys

Building Contractors

Building Materials

What Type of Business Is for Me?

Experience & Skills

Rate 1 (Low) to 10 (High)

Experience & Skills	Antiques	Auto Parts	Auto Repairs	Bakery	Beauty Shop	Café/Restaurant	Caterer	Clothing	Cocktails	Coffee Shop	Dentist	Donut Shop	Drug Store	Fast Food	Florist	Furniture	Service Stn.	Gifts	Ice Cream	Jewelry	Laundry (Coin)	Music Shop	Pizza	Pet Shop	Photography	Rock Shop	Tailor	Trucking	Retail	Wholesale	Other
Management																															
Finance																															
Law																															
Supervision																															
Negotiator																															
Instructor																															
Advertisement																															
Promoter																															
Educator																															
Leader																															
Personnel																															
Purchaser																															
Sales Mgr.																															
Service																															
Product Developer																															
Organizer																															
Credit Evaluator																															
Collector																															
Decision-Maker																															
Perseverance																															
Physical Energy																															
Public Relations																															
Total:																															

Business Suggestions *(Continued)*

Bus Lines	Gasoline Service Stations
Cafes	Gifts
Camera Shops	Greeting Cards
Carpenters	Groceries/Markets
x Carpet Cleaners	Hamburger Stands
Carpet Sales	Hardware Stores
Caterers	Health Clubs
Clothing Stores	Heating-Air Condition Shops
Cocktail Lounges	Hobby Shops
Coffee Shops	Horse Rental
x Coin Laundries	Hot Dog Stands
Costume Shops	Ice Cream Shops
Dairy Drive-Ins	Insurance Agencies
Dance Studios	Interior Decorators
Delicatessen	Janitorial Services
Dentists	Jewelry Shops
Dinner Houses	Jobbers
Dog Grooming	Kennel Clubs
Donut Shops	Liquor Stores
Distributorships	Machine Shops
Driving Ranges	Masonry Workers
Drug Stores	Maternity Shops
Dry Cleaners	Medical Laboratories
Electricians	Motels
Employment Agencies	Moving Companies
Engineers	Music Shops/Schools
Exterminators	News Stands
Farms	Nightclubs
Fast Foods	Nurseries (Plants)
Fire Alarm Systems	Nursery Schools
Fisheries	Nursing Homes
Floor Covering Stores	Office Supplies & Equipment
Florists	Optometrists
Funeral Parlors	Pest Control
Furniture Stores	Pet Shops
x Garden Supplies (Vegetables)	Paint Stores

Business Suggestions *(Continued)*

x Photography Studios
   Picture Framing Stores
   Pizza Shops
   Pool Services
x Print Shops (small)
   Real Estate Agencies
   Record Stores
   Restaurants
   Riding Stables
   Rock Shops
   Roller Rinks
   Roofers
   Sandwich Shops
   Scientific Equipment Stores
   Secretarial Services
   Sheet Metal Fabricators
x Shoe Repairs
   Sign & Display Suppliers
   Ski Shops

Small Contractors
Snack Bars
Surveyors
Sweeping Services
Swim Schools
Tailors
Taverns
Taxi Services
Theaters
Title Companies
Travel Agencies
Trucking Firms
Variety Stores
Vending Routes
Veterinarians
Wedding Chapels
Welders
Wholesalers

Management?

Do you have managerial skills? Have you ever held a position where these skills were required? If so, why not cash in on your experience and start a business in which you are the manager, the boss of the whole show. To be a good manager you must know how to handle people who work for you. Your attitude toward your employees is important. To be an effective manager you must have practical skill when dealing with people and their problems. Be confident in your own abilities and be aware of what you are doing. Employees can soon unmask a "phony" and they will take advantage of you!

It is not an easy job to manage people. It is done by trial and error and there will probably be a lot of errors before you finally become a top manager, even in your own business.

Learn to understand people and find out why they do certain things. Keep in mind always that your own self-esteem is important and that you are running *your* business for a profit, not as a philanthropic society for the welfare of your employees. Of course, if your business is successful your employees will benefit. This is what you have to impart to them—that the harder they work to improve the business the better off they will be, because conditions will be better and there will be raises and maybe bonuses in a prosperous organization. Never promise anything you do not intend to do at some future date.

The people who work for you have desires and ambitions even though to you their wishes may appear insignificant. Remember too that they have their own private lives. Often you must make concessions so that they have some free time for special purposes with their families and friends.

A good manager should listen to employees' time-saving and other ideas; a reward is a good incentive for an employee who comes up with a time-saving idea. Take time out to listen to employees' proposals and if there are differences of opinions, as there will be, talk to the employee or employees and straighten things out before these small problems become larger unsolvable ones.

In other words, as a good manager you are like a parent, even though you may be young. People will look to you for advice and assistance and often you will be a listening post for their family problems or personal successes. Give a little of your time to those who need it, but don't overdo it. If you feel that some employees are taking advantage of you and your time, just tell them that you too have family problems, but the business place is not where you air your worries. Treat them gently but firmly; if necessary transfer them to another part of the organization if they become too "chatty."

As your business grows encourage your employees to participate in decision-making. Let them become leaders in their own right when they are trained well enough to take over such a position.

Selling?

Are you good at selling? Have you thought about going into a business where your main job would be to sell your products either directly or via salespeople?

To be a good salesperson you should consider several points:

1. Learn how to eliminate your competitors by emphasizing the exclusive benefits of your product or service. Be prepared to study your product thoroughly before attempting to market it or to train other salespersons to sell it. Once you have proved to a prospect the benefits of your product over that of a competitor, then your job is partially finished.

2. You should *not* make promises you know you cannot keep. Present your product in a logical way, building up the prospect's interest and wish to purchase your product. You must be convincing—what you are offering is what the prospect needs. Once this is done, another hurdle has been crossed. When you are training others as salespeople, why not tape a presentation so the trainees can hear what a good sales pitch is before they go out into the marketplace cold.

3. Be honest with your claims. Your story must be believable. Don't exaggerate the benefits to be achieved by using your product. Don't downplay your competition in a mean way, especially if you know your prospect has been selling your competitor's product for many years—successfully.

4. Once you have convinced your prospect to order from you, ask for the order outright. Don't give your prospect the chance to say "I'll call you in ten days." By that time the prospect will have forgotten all about your product as well as your sales pitch. Do your best to clinch the deal while the message is still "hot." Of course, you cannot always get an order that quickly, but try! If you have given the prospect all the facts honestly and have pointed out all the advantages of purchasing your product over that of your competition, then keep on asking for the order. Very often the beginning salesperson who is not courageous enough to close a deal dilly-dallies

and does not start writing up the order until the prospect finally says yes. Sometimes "yes" does not come because the prospect has become fed up with this wishy-washy salesperson.

5. As you, the salesperson, go through your talk make sure that the prospect agrees with the points you raise. If the prospect hesitates to give you an affirmative answer to some of your questions, reword them. Get an affirmative reply before you go on to your next statement about your product and its benefits.

6. When you have finished your pitch start writing up the order for whatever it is you have to sell. Fill in the order form and get the prospect to read and sign on the dotted line. A good "closing" is often more important than the sales pitch itself.

To be a good sales manager you have to master all of the above techniques in selling. If you as sales manager find that your trainees are not following your instructions on how to sell and close a sale, reprimand them once or twice; if they continue to disobey your training orders, fire them! This action is in your best interest.

Sometimes a salesperson needs visual aids. These should be supplied by the home office. Visual aids keep the salesperson and the sales pitch up-to-date on the product or service.

Public Relations?

Do you have any public relations experience? This work covers a multitude of fields: for example, speech writing, syndicated columns on various topics for newspapers and magazines, advertising, promoting products, and radio and television commercials and scripts. These are just a few ideas to get you thinking.

If you did not enjoy your prior work in public relations—perhaps that was the reason you quit your job—then *do not go into a similar business,* because it will fail. Do something you enjoy and you will *succeed.*

Let's take a few examples of public relations work and see what is entailed. Many of the most important public relations efforts are done by publicity writers who have to find the proper platform for a speech. They often end up writing the speeches themselves, since few executives can write their own speeches. A large proportion of publicity writers employed by corporations and other agencies are today engaged in speech-writing as well as in publicizing speeches. There will be a big demand for this type of work in your own public relations business.

In-house newsletters are another form of public relations work. These letters can be in the form of pamphlets or booklets, or they may be just straightforward letters. These are often prepared and edited in the PR department of a company with help from other departments like personnel. They can also be prepared by a PR consulting company, often more cheaply than by the staff of a large business concern.

The fields of radio, TV, and motion pictures are not always thought of as publicity media; however, there are hundreds of publicity writers who concentrate on these outlets. They prepare scripts or parts of scripts to be included in the programs.

Another suggestion is to write a column and try to get it syndicated. There are many large syndicates and the names and addresses can be found in any library.

Or you can work as a "stringer" for a newspaper or a magazine or both. Stringers are persons who find interesting pieces of news or who are assigned stories to write up for the news media. There's not much money in it, but it may prove worthwhile as a part-time job if you like to write.

You can design pamphlets advertising products for certain companies, do layouts and get camera-ready materials to printers, handing over the finished products to your clients.

Some companies need reports—quarterly, half-yearly, and annually. You can offer to do this work for them by setting up a small typing bureau.

There are endless opportunities in public relations. They should be researched thoroughly before you decide which program you would like to enter. It is interesting work. You will meet different kinds of people from all walks of life. If you like people this could be the work for you.

Leadership?

Do you have the ability to become a good leader? If so, you should go into the type of business that requires this ability. Let me ask you— what is a good leader? The answer is, one who can be described as a guide, a commander, one who can take charge without offending people.

There are several questions you should ask yourself to determine whether or not you are a leader or can become one: (1) Do you have a following? (2) Are your followers a voluntary group or did you have to persuade them to follow you? (3) Can you tell people the best way to get things done and have them do it *your* way? (4) Do you consider yourself the best person to do a particular job in a certain situation? A leader should be a model for others to follow. People will only follow you as long as you can prove to them that you know what you are doing and are doing it to the best of your ability.

To be a leader in these times, a good education is not enough. You may have all the degrees offered and still not be a good leader. To guide others you must constantly be learning and developing your own self-image. You must add to your knowledge and to your skills daily. Another point to remember—budget your time and do not waste it. Leave enough time to concentrate on your business and to build up confidence among your fellow workers.

Show your employees by example how they too can become leaders. Don't expect them to always follow in your footsteps—it is up to you to show them the way to head up departments—to be commanders in their own right. Once you have guided them over the rough spots in an organization don't leave them floundering. Give them responsibilities and be free to further improve yourself and your company.

Organization?

Are you a good organizer? Can you organize a business or set up a corporation? If so, you can (1) be a "professional organizer," that is, set up companies for other persons, or (2) set up your own business. The following information will help in either of the above circumstances.

If you have the capital and the business know-how you can start a small business or corporation from scratch. This may be better than buying a ready-made organization where sales may be low due to prior bad management. As an organizer you must set up policies which have to be followed without any deviations, unless discussed with you first.

On the other hand, if you can reorganize a business that has already been started and improve it, it may turn into a more profitable venture than trying to start a business fresh.

Your organizing abilities will come in handy if you plan to employ either inside or outside salespeople to work for you. You must organize sales training programs so that employees know, among other details, how long it takes to get a product delivered or manufactured, how to promote sales, and all about your accounting system. Salespeople must be familiar with all phases of your business. Company policy must be set down on paper and each person on your sales staff must get a copy.

Remember, an owner of a business is not only the organizer of the venture but often the sole proprietor and must see to it that everything is handled correctly so the business will make a profit. Treat all personnel kindly but firmly; then your employees, once trained in *your* business, won't seek other employment!

Buying?

What about experience in buying? Have you ever held a purchasing position? Did you enjoy it? If the answer is yes, you might set up an organization where you buy wholesale and sell to retailers. For this business you have to have a fairly substantial amount of capital. Until you can establish a good credit line, many suppliers will want cash when supplying you with products for resale. And your clients may want thirty to sixty days credit! You may also require a truck or van for delivery unless the goods can be shipped by rail or interstate truck to your clients.

Before you finally decide to be a purchaser, research the need for products in your area; then decide which type of goods you want to handle. Let's take for example seasonal items. These would have to be shipped at specific times of the year, so that they arrive in time for the retailer to sell. Christmas goods that arrive around Easter would not be acceptable to anybody and you would get a bad name for being unreliable. Therefore, before you decide on this type of business you must locate good suppliers for your product and make sure they deliver at the requested time. Always, of course, ask for delivery well within the selling season so that you get your products to the retailers in time for them to set up their displays. Be sure that there is a return clause for damaged goods, otherwise you may be out of business if too many things are broken or do not work. Mechanical items must be completely guaranteed by the manufacturer. These products can be faulty and not function correctly.

WHAT ARE MY NEEDS?

The next consideration—What are my needs? That is, what do I require in order to succeed in my new business? Go through the accompanying table and rate yourself 1 (low) to 10 (high) on each item. Then add up the totals under the types of business and opposite each of your needs. This will help you evaluate what is required before you go into your own business.

The following examples should assist you when going over your basic needs before starting up your business.

Capital to Operate

Under the heading "Capital—Operating" you will have to decide how much money is needed to run your chosen business successfully. Having your own business can be very rewarding mentally and financially if it is run properly. You must be prepared to work hard.

What Are My Needs?

Needs
Rate 1 (Low) to 10 (High)

	Antiques	Auto Parts	Auto Repairs	Bakery	Beauty Shop	Café/Restaurant	Caterer	Clothing	Cocktails	Coffee Shop	Dentist	Donut Shop	Drug Store	Fast Food	Florist	Furniture	Service Stn.	Gifts	Ice Cream	Jewelry	Laundry (Coin)	Music Shop	Pizza	Pet Shop	Photography	Rock Shop	Tailor	Trucking	Retail	Wholesale	Other
Capital—Operating																															
Capital—Living																															
Tax Shelter																															
Recession-proof																															
Risk																															
Appreciation																															
Depreciation																															
Leverage																															
Work Capacity																															
Seasonal																															
Days																															
Weeks																															
Hours																															
Employees																															
Relatives																															
Partners																															
Total:																															

If your family can help you in the beginning it would reduce your work load. Then when you have to be away from them for longer periods than you did when you worked at a regular job, they will understand that they will benefit in the long run.

Remember, even if you purchase an established business, machinery or other equipment may need renovating or replacing, if not immediately then at some later date. Put aside sufficient cash for emergencies, like machinery breakdown. There will be a need for initial inventory purchases to make your business look presentable. It is important to show old and new customers that you are here to stay and that you have plenty of stock on hand to meet their needs. All this takes money! Plan on it!

Installation fees for telephones—they may have to be relocated—utility installation fees, taxes and licenses, stationery and other supply costs all have to be considered in your budget. Also, the services of an accountant will be needed at the end of the accounting year. You may need the services of an attorney or a consultant to advise you on certain points in your business.

There are expenses for advertising and insurance premiums. (It is very important that you carry sufficient insurance in a business in case of injury, fire, etc.) There may be dues to unions or other organizations that you need to join in order to be "in" among the neighborhood businesses. There may also be travel expenses. All these monies must be put aside for use prior to starting up your business—even before you open up your doors to the public.

You can see that a good amount of capital is needed for operational expenses. Financing can be obtained from various sources. (See Chapter 7 for further information on this subject.) Make sure that the rate of return on your capital expenditure shows that you made a good investment, or at least a better investment than some other you might have chosen.

Taxes

Another thing to investigate before you get into a business is how you will be taxed. What licenses and permits if any will be needed? In most cases the IRS can help you. However, make sure that you do not visit their offices during their busy tax season. Go and see them when they have time to spend explaining things to you. Or you can consult a tax attorney or accountant, but that will cost you money.

Capital for Personal Living

A year's living expenses should be saved up before you attempt to go into business, for the simple reason that it may take about that time to show any profit in your business. Your family must go on living even if your company takes some time to show a financial gain.

Make a list of all necessary expenses such as mortgage payments, taxes, utilities, groceries, entertainment, and so on. Try to live within your budget.

Be prepared to purchase new tools and equipment in a business. These can be depreciated over a certain number of years. Your accountant will take care of this tax deduction when completing your annual tax return. If you purchase an established business, there may be old equipment which will need immediate replacement. The outlay may be large but the depreciation tax write-off can also be large due to hard wear and short life on what you purchase for the business. It may pay to purchase new items and depreciate them over a period of time, rather than to try to work with old run-down equipment.

Partnership

If you decide to take in a partner—and this can be good or bad—a lot depends on who you choose to help you run your business. A good partnership can be valuable in many ways. One way is that your cash flow will be stronger if your partner brings in some money. Another important factor—you could take more time off if there were a responsible person to look after the business in your absence. The same applies to the partner.

If you choose a partner who is not congenial then there can be all sorts of trouble. It is somewhat difficult to find out in advance how a person will react to some of your suggestions and vice versa! The choice is yours, whether you wish to work alone, form a partnership, set up a corporation, or just employ persons to work in the business with you on a daily basis. Relatives brought into a business as partners often cause friction, usually due to jealousy. If things do not work out there can be family problems.

Employees

When you have employees, their hours must be strictly adhered to. Do you want them to work a full week, part-time, or by the hour? How many days a week? It is best to get everything in writing and signed by each party, then there can be little cause for confusion at a later date. It may sound petty to get everything down in writing, but you will save yourself a lot of headaches if you do, and it prevents trouble.

You must know how each person works. Is your employee physically strong? If there are heavy packages can they be lifted by your employees or by yourself? Take into consideration every phase of the business and talk it over thoroughly with your workers and partners so that at a later date there is no argument about who is responsible for what activity. It is important, of course, to prevent substandard performance on the part of your employees or yourself to prevent unnecessary expenses due to bad management.

Seasonal Business

If your chosen business is seasonal and you have to hire personnel to help you out in your busy times, make sure that they are good workers. Do not keep anybody on the job if they do not do a full day's work when you are paying them good wages. However, don't be on their backs all the time. Many good employees object to this kind of treatment and you will get more complaints and less work done. Be kind but strict. Enforce your regulations, not with an iron hand but with a firm hand!

LOCATION! LOCATION! LOCATION!

The success or failure of your business venture depends heavily on traffic. One of your first priorities before buying is to make sure the business location is attractive. Will your business be located on a side street where too few cars pass and few people would see you? Will it be hidden in a corner of a shopping mall where people do not have to pass by? Will it be on a country road where few tourists drive? These days many businesses depend on automobile traffic, therefore it is important that your business is situated where this kind of traffic has easy access.

Automobile traffic can be divided roughly into three categories:

1. The customer traveling to work likes to find dry cleaners and drug stores on the right-hand side of the road. On the way to work this person can stop briefly and still easily get back into the traffic flow. On the way home from work, a worker prefers to have a market on the "going-home" side of the road. This potential customer can pick up items for the evening meal or do a week's shopping and then slide back into the traffic flow.

2. A customer on a planned shopping expedition likes to shop in a larger area where there are a number of stores and where prices can be compared. This type of customer is more casual and has more time to spend. Before settling on your location, see if there are any stores similar to the one you propose to open in the vicinity. If there are too many like stores in one place, they rarely prosper.

3. A pleasure trip often entails stopping somewhere for the night. Tired drivers do *not* want to drive for miles after leaving the highway to find a motel or a gas station.

To help you choose a suitable location we suggest you check your local banks, trade associations, suppliers, and the Small Business Administration for any information they can give you about the activities in a particular area. City Hall, the local Chamber of Commerce, and the Better Business Bureau can offer valuable information on the size of the population (Is it growing or shrinking?) as well as the amount of auto and foot traffic near your planned location.

The type of business you plan to open depends upon the type of population in the area. For instance, a heavily industrialized area may not be a good place for a bookstore. On the other hand, a town or city with one or more colleges or a university should be ideal for a bookstore, a bar and grill, a sporting goods outlet, or a recreational facility.

Is there a military base nearby? Military personnel and their families can be a steady source of business, providing that the item you are selling cannot be purchased at substantial government discount at the base PX!

What kind of tourist attractions are near your business site? Are they seasonal or year round? Does the area in which you plan to buy your business have good newspapers and radio or television stations? These are important considerations for advertising purposes!

The type of people passing your store can be divided into three categories:

1. **Browsers** These "lookers" occasionally buy. They like to shop around before they buy anything. They may come back some weeks later and purchase an item, or they may never return. The store owner needs courteous salespersons to entice customers to buy without feeling any high-pressure sales tactics. Customers who do not buy on the first visit will feel comfortable returning at a later date. For example, if you have a real estate business you will find that some clients are not necessarily looking for a new home; they are trying to get some ideas on how to renovate their own house! A good salesperson knows how to weed out these lookers. Experience will tell you, and so will your hired help, who are buyers themselves. Always be friendly because sooner or later these lookers will probably buy something!

2. **Passers-by** If you have a store with a window display, make it attractive so that passers-by will want to enter and purchase some merchandise. You can often get this type of customer into your place of business by an attractive outside display; and they sometimes buy! However, passers-by may be people on their way to or from work. Your window display should let them know what you sell when they need your product. Hopefully they will remember your store as a supply source for their needs.

3. **Buyers**   What makes a person enter and buy? People who enter
and buy either have heard about your store or need something
that you sell. Perhaps your window display attracted them at some
time in the past. There are many ways to get people into your
place of business. See to it that they do not walk out empty-
handed! Many shoppers like to enter a store and purchase things
they need that are on display. They do not have to rummage
around to find the item they need. People recommend to their
friends to shop at certain places. Of course, the personnel in any
business should be polite and helpful at all times. Don't let a
salesperson persuade a customer to buy something the customer
does not really need just to make a sale or because the item is on
sale. The customer may buy this time but may never return because of the pushy salesperson. A "soft sell" is the best sell!

According to the Small Business Administration, ". . . information
gathered about the passing traffic should include counting the individuals who seem to possess the characteristics appropriate to the
desired clientele, judging their reasons for using that route, and
calculating their ability to buy." In other words, take the time to check
out the type of people in the area in which you intend to open your
own business.

There are many other locational factors to take into account before
you open up a business. One is its access to major highways, airports,
train and bus depots, and freight terminals. Not only do potential
customers need easy access, but also your suppliers appreciate it too.
Ample parking is another plus for customers and suppliers.

GOOD TIMES AND BAD TIMES

Look into a recession-proof business—one that will prosper regardless of the economy. Reread the list of businesses given at the beginning of this chapter and pay special attention to the ones marked
with an *x*, since they usually do well in an inflationary economy. Also
look at the categories listed in the table for additional ideas for businesses in slack times. Often a hobby can be turned into an excellent
business, depending on the times.

If a recession comes, the following are just a few types of businesses that are worth looking into. People turn to businesses that help keep, for example, an old car running or old equipment working. When times are tough, the general public prefers a good used piece of merchandise rather than a new product that costs too much money. People have to keep their clothes clean and tidy, so cleaners prosper in a recession. Household furniture and electrical appliances are used longer than usual, therefore upholsterers are needed, along with people who can repair appliances.

Why do certain businesses do better in a recession? Here are some examples—in addition to the ones mentioned above.

1. Thrift shops sell more to a different type of person than they would in normal times. For example, large families have to keep their children warm in winter and cool in summer. If there is unemployment or low income due to hard times, parents will go to a thrift store to purchase clothes rather than to a retail shop.

2. Automobile repair is necessary. Old cars are kept longer in a family and as a consequence they require more repairs. Auto repair stores do good business in bad times.

3. Coin laundries thrive. By taking laundry to coin-operated machines, money is saved as well as time, because more than one machine can be working for the user. Saving time can become important when both husband and wife are working full time. Time is important to the working person.

4. Small-time printers do well in time of recession because, to survive, businesses must advertise their wares. It is cheaper to print flyers than to advertise in the local newspapers. Local young people can deliver flyers door to door.

TYPES OF BUSINESSES

You should have a solid idea of what type of business you want to buy. In general, there are four main business categories:

1. Retail   3. Manufacturing

2. Wholesale   4. Service

In addition, businesses may be spread over an economic scale according to the amount of capital necessary to acquire and operate them.

Hobby (Small net)		Restaurant (Medium net)		Manufacturing (Large net)
$0–10 K	$50 K	$100 K	$500 K	$1 M+

The business you choose will be determined by your personal background and experience, your desire to own a business, what you *want* to do, your strengths and weaknesses (discussed in Chapter 1), your attitudes toward "risk," and your financial resources. Do a thorough investigation and analysis of your potential market in order to determine your marketing strategy, organizational plan, and financial objectives.

Risk

There is a risk in starting up a new business, so buying a going concern is sometimes better than starting from scratch, providing it is what you want and the price is right. Don't go in for something you hate just because it appears to be an easy way to earn money. You must have a "feel" for the business, as well as enough capital so that you and your family will not starve to death waiting to make a profit! Opportunities can be found through advertisements in newspapers and in trade publications. Some realtors specialize in selling small businesses.

Just because an old business is run down does not mean that a new person running the store could not boost sales by hard work. A run-down store or business is often sold cheaply. If rebuilding the business seems feasible it may be worth buying. This is an individual choice.

Buying a business involves a lot of time and money with no guarantee of a return for your efforts. However, future profit is the most important thing to look for, so if you can see a good future in what you want to purchase, by all means buy it. (See Chapter 4 for more on this subject.)

Merchandise

Now we come to the type of merchandise you want to sell. Are you interested in convenience items such as milk, bread, and cigarettes or High Unit priced goods such as automobiles, boats, and appliances? Or do you wish to go into a specialty business selling for instance brand-name photographic or stereo equipment?

All of these businesses require a careful choice of location because the type of customer for each business varies; for example, convenience stores are usually on a corner near a main road where people can enter and park easily. These stores should also be near residential areas. High Unit priced goods do better in a shopping center near large department stores where customers can compare prices without too much traveling.

Specialty Shops

"Specialty" clients know and like certain brands, and so the location of this kind of store can be in a shopping center where other specialty shops are located—not of course selling the same type of goods that you plan to sell. The specialty shop does not have to be located near a big department store. Clients who are fussy about what they purchase will always look for their brand, even if the store is at the other end of the mall!

FINANCIAL RESOURCES

After you have selected the type of business that suits you and your business needs and have considered other factors like location and the economy, narrow down your list of potential businesses to say three:

1. _____

2. _____

3. _____

Estimated Monthly Expenses

Item	Your estimate of monthly expenses based on sales of $_____ per year	Your estimate of how much cash you need to start your business (See column 3.)	What to put in column 2 (These figures are typical for one kind of business. You will have to decide how many months to allow for in your business.)
	Column 1 $	Column 2 $	Column 3
Salary of owner-manager			2 times column 1
All other salaries and wages			3 times column 1
Rent			3 times column 1
Advertising			3 times column 1
Delivery expense			3 times column 1
Supplies			3 times column 1
Telephone and telegraph			3 times column 1
Other utilities			3 times column 1
Insurance			Payment required by insurance company.
Taxes, including Social Security			4 times column 1

Interest	3 times column 1
Maintenance	3 times column 1
Legal and other professional fees	3 times column 1
Miscellaneous	3 times column 1
Starting Costs You Only Have to Pay Once	Leave column 2 blank
Fixtures and equipment	Fill in worksheet on page 40 and put the total here.
Decorating and remodeling	Talk it over with a contractor.
Installation of fixtures and equipment	Talk to suppliers from whom you buy these.
Starting inventory	Suppliers will probably help you estimate this.
Deposits with public utilities	Find out from utility companies.
Legal and other professional fees	Lawyer, accountant, and so on.
Licenses and permits	Find out from city offices what you have to have.

Estimated Monthly Expenses

Item	Your estimate of monthly expenses based on sales of $_____ per year	Your estimate of how much cash you need to start your business (See column 3.)	What to put in column 2 (These figures are typical for one kind of business. You will have to decide how many months to allow for in your business.)
	Column 1	Column 2	
Advertising and promotion for opening			Column 3 Estimate what you'll use.
Accounts receivable			What you need to buy more stock until credit customers pay.
Cash			For unexpected expenses or losses, special purchases, etc.
Other			Make a separate list and enter total.
Total Estimated Cash You Need to Start With		$	Add up all the numbers in column 2.

Now determine your financial resources:

1. Cash on hand (cash and savings) $ _____

2. Assets (borrowed against real property:
   house, insurance policy, auto, stocks and
   bonds, securities, valuables, etc.) $ _____

3. Bank credit (personal loans) $ _____

4. Borrowed (from relatives and friends) $ _____

Remember to keep some of your money in reserve for unforeseen expenses and for additional operating capital. *Don't get caught short!*

Now that you have decided on the amount of cash you have available, the next step is to decide what your expenses will be. The Small Business Administration (SBA) suggests the breakdown of expenses in the accompanying worksheet. Some of the items mentioned in this worksheet may not be applicable, but the list of items is very complete and well worth studying. Look at Chapter 7 for further finance information for your business opportunity.

By now you should have a good estimate of how much money you have to work with, and should have thoroughly investigated the risks you must take in your venture.

If you are purchasing a well-established business, you will find another SBA suggested worksheet helpful. This list covers items you may purchase from the previous owner, or those that may be necessary to buy. Often some of these items like display cabinets and storage shelves can be bought used or from a discount house at a reasonable cost.

After you have studied this chapter thoroughly, we recommend you reassess your qualifications honestly. Can you change your attitudes, gain needed skills, overcome bad habits, and alter work routines to fit the business you want to buy? If so, you should be a successful business person!

List of Furniture, Fixtures, and Equipment

Leave out or add items to suit your business. Use separate sheets to list exactly what you need for each of the items below.	If you plan to pay cash in full, enter full amount below and in the last column.	If you are going to pay by installments, fill out the columns below. Enter in the last column your down payment plus at least one installment.			Estimate of the cash you need for furniture, fixtures, and equipment.
		Price	Down payment	Amount of each installment	
Counters	$	$	$	$	$
Storage shelves, cabinets					
Display stands, shelves, tables					
Cash register					
Safe					
Window display fixtures					
Special lighting					
Outside sign					
Delivery equipment if needed					
Total Furniture, Fixtures, and Equipment					$

3

How and Where to Look for a Business

It's surprising! When we ask people where they would look for business opportunities, most of them shrug their shoulders. Yet business is all around. You can find it everywhere. One place to start is the list of business opportunity leads at the end of this chapter.

Another suggestion: Talk with people. People create business and businesses. Don't be shy. Most people avoid direct contact with strangers because they fear appearing stupid or bold and abrasive, or they fear being rejected. To succeed in business—indeed, to succeed in finding the right type of business—you must be able to deal effectively with a variety of people. If you are planning to buy a quick-copy print business, don't talk to a hot-dog-stand owner! But if you want to buy a hot dog stand you will definitely need to talk with the following people: hot-dog-stand owners, suppliers, lenders, advertisers, equipment manufacturers, and—hot dog eaters!

APPROACHING THE OWNER

When you approach an owner, ask intelligent questions! Asking a hot-dog-stand owner how long it takes to cook a hot dog isn't going to get you very far! Inquire if the owner is considering selling. Perhaps the owner is doing well and is happy but may know of other hot dog stands for sale. The owner may be able to tell you of a possibly excellent location for a stand, or who the best, most reliable suppliers are in the area. Ask! You'll get the answers you need.

One good tip: Dress casually. Don't turn off the owner and employees by looking like an investigator for the IRS. Creating unwarranted suspicion is the surest way to develop a poor relationship with an owner who is a valuable source of information for you.

Perhaps you feel uncomfortable approaching the owner of a business "cold turkey." Check the listings in your local newspaper—the "Business for Sale" ads. Write letters to owners whose businesses are for sale, or to those who might sell eventually. Letter-writing is slower and less effective than in-person interviews, but it may bring results. If all else fails, place an advertisement in your local newspaper. Post notices on community bulletin boards. Offer a reward for information!

Remember, the time you spend looking for a business is your own. Budget it wisely. Keep records of businesses you visit. Take notes on what happens during your interviews with owners. A tape recorder can be very useful, with the interviewee's consent, of course. Work when you have the most energy, when you feel fresh. Early morning and evening might be better than during the late afternoon doldrums when the business day is coming to a close. Make a list of whom you perceive to be the most important people to see and interview them first. Telephone ahead to be sure they will be in when you get there. Set a goal: Try to see one or two owners a day and make several appointments. List a variety of places to contact in advance so you know how your time will be spent.

No doubt you will encounter stumbling blocks when talking with some owners. They may not disclose their goals or plans for the future because they do not want the community to know about important personal decisions. Let's review some of the common objections from the "War Story Chest" to illustrate why an owner cannot or will not tell you everything during an interview.

First, the owner may be uncertain how to sell the business. The potential seller may be unaware of business, government, and professional codes, as well as other laws, rules, and regulations required in business opportunity transactions, and therefore may hedge about any talk of selling the business. As a potential buyer, however, you may help by pointing out the complete procedural checklist system necessary to assure a complete business opportunity transaction.

The owner may tell you, "No, I am definitely not interested in selling." Perhaps it has been several months or nearly a year since the owner made a self-evaluation or an evaluation of the business. Is the owner spending too much time running it? When was the owner's last vacation? How much family time has the owner allowed for? Has the owner estimated his or her hourly wage or "true net profit"? How much stress does the owner cope with each day? Does the owner have to hassle with employees, customers, vendors, and others? If the owner admits to you "honestly" his or her true feelings, you may find the owner is closer to selling the business than either of you thought!

Perhaps the owner won't disclose specific information about the business because of a reluctance simply to divulge recipes, trade secrets, or operating techniques. You must build up the owner's confidence and trust. Reveal to the owner that you are a friend and a potential buyer, not a competitor, supplier, or the IRS!

In conclusion, your ability to find a business is based on the knowledge you already possess and the knowledge you gain from talking with individuals directly involved in their own businesses. Don't be afraid to be inquisitive. Find out where the best business is for you by seeking out the best businesses and business people! If you still feel uncomfortable making calls "cold turkey," writing letters, or telephoning, then call a professional broker. (See Chapter 19.)

IDENTIFYING BUSINESS OPPORTUNITIES

To buy or sell a business, check the following sources for potential clients. There are directories of these business opportunity leads in most libraries.

Referrals

Buyers

Sellers

Landlords

Attorneys

Accountants

Bankers

Management consultants

Stockholders

Owner advertisements

Better Business Bureau

Chamber of Commerce

Old listings (Multiple Listing Service)

Contacts Influential Directory

Telephone books

Business directories

Newspapers

Certified business counselors

National business opportunities marketing meetings

Exchange meetings

Trade journals

Associations

Libraries

Small Business Administration

U.S. Printing Office

Distributors

Certified business opportunity appraisers (CBOA)

4

Should
I Buy an
Existing Business?

In deciding whether to buy an existing business or to start a new one from scratch, you will see that there are a variety of advantages and disadvantages on either side. The purpose of this chapter is to discuss the positive and negative aspects of each venture, and to reveal to you why many people fail because they did not prepare sufficiently for as great an undertaking as going into business for themselves.

EXISTING BUSINESS BENEFITS

First of all, if you plan to buy an existing business, there will be no start-up delay—unless of course you plan to rip out all the equipment and start from "square one"! Most businesses for sale are usually in good shape as far as equipment and decor are concerned. Consequently, you can open your business the same day you buy it and establish an immediate cash flow.

Furthermore, the business's name, good will, and reputation are known, and there is therefore an established clientele. Yesterday's customers are tomorrow's customers. Your accounts are established. You have something on which to build. In addition, operating knowledge and procedures will be handed over with the business. This means that suppliers are established; many of the experimental aspects of the business have been eliminated; past profits or loss and credit are known. And, finally, you won't have large advertising expenses because the business is already known to the community.

Most of the disadvantages of buying an existing business can be known before a purchase is made. For instance, by asking people in the community or by going to other sources of local information as discussed in Chapter 2—such as the City Hall and Chamber of Commerce—and finding out about the business's reputation. If it's bad, trouble lies ahead. Unless you are supremely confident in your public relations ability, a business with a bad reputation can ruin the self-confidence you need to perform all the tasks required of business ownership.

Another factor to consider is loss of revenue. If a business is losing money when it is put up for sale, there could be a variety of reasons all pointing to danger for the next owner. Use the guidelines discussed in Chapter 3 to ascertain why the business is losing money. It could be a bad location or poor business practices which are contributing to the owner's loss.

Perhaps the business has been run into the ground. Old equipment, peeling paint, and outmoded lighting and interior design are definite signs of a sliding business—perhaps a sliding reputation as well! Look in the corners and on the shelves. Does the inventory look old, dusty, worn out?

ESTABLISHING A NEW BUSINESS

It is more difficult to establish a brand new business. There is certainly a higher risk involved. However, a new business may fill a need in the community. Establishing the need for a new business will require a lot more effort and research on your part. Although there may be a need, the cash base may not exist in the community. The result may be failure. Thorough research to establish the need and cash availability of your business is a must!

When you start a new business you have the fun of trying new procedures, ideas, and concepts. Experimentation can be exciting and profitable when you establish ideas that work. The community too will no doubt support and help you find what works best for themselves and for you too! Because you are starting from scratch, your equipment and other furnishings are new. Machines, refrigerated cases, and so on are less likely to break down; so upkeep and repair work will not be a factor.

However, the disadvantages can sometimes be overwhelming for the new owner. A new business needs time to grow, to establish a name and a reputation. You must expect higher than normal advertising costs for the first one to three years. Moreover, start-up time may be long, tedious, or endlessly delayed. First, you will have to find a suitable location. After that, obtaining zoning and building permits and licenses could take time, especially if your business requires that state and local requirements are met you will need to look for suppliers, set up business procedures, and develop operating strategies. All this could take many weeks or months!

Be prepared to spend time, energy, and—*money!* You may not see a return on your investment for a long time. Can you afford to wait for success? The costs required for starting a new business are much higher, and the credit limits will be much lower. In addition, you will be spending longer hours at your business for the first one to two years. Remember too that it is more difficult for a new business to establish a competitive position than it is for an established business to maintain its competitive position through an ownership change.

The result—the "bottom line"—is, of course, that in a new business there is less profit during the first year or two. Chances are there may be no profit at all! So, if you are fortunate enough to possess the skills, abilities, and characteristics discussed and scored by you in Chapter 1, you should first consider buying a going business and second, consider a new business.

SELLER'S CLAIMS

You can see from the preceding sections that there is a strong case for buying an existing business, or at least for adopting one on which to build if what you want exists in the community. Make sure to check why the business is for sale. Is it declining? Is there an expiring lease? Are the products, facilities, or need for the services obsolete? Is there new and better competition? Is the location in the way of new highway construction?

In almost every case the seller will claim to be sick, retiring, or interested in another business. Be very wary. Only one out of twenty sellers is really sick, retiring, or with other business interests. Most likely the seller is sick—sick and tired of operating a business that's losing money and profits! So most owners will welcome any reasonable offer that will free them from the responsibilities that have become burdensome.

Remember, most people fail because they simply are not prepared for ownership. There are five basic reasons for their failure.

1. They procrastinate. They put off today what they feel can be done in the future. The business of business is "busy-ness." Don't waste time.

2. They neglect to establish a financial goal. This can lead to discouragement and failure. Know what you want and aim for it.

3. They fail to consult a real estate broker, an attorney, and accountant—which may lead to bankruptcy, lawsuits, or financial ruin. Even though you are confident about your abilities, don't second guess. Get a second or third opinion. Seek a professional's help.

4. They don't succeed because they may not adhere to local, state, and federal guidelines on zoning and tax laws.

5. They fail because of ignorance of the procedures discussed in "How to Buy and Sell Business Opportunities" by American Business Consultants, Inc.

You now have the basic information on businesses to look for and are aware of the positive and negative aspects of buying either an established business or a brand new one. In the following chapters we will discuss in more detail the risk-taking and the financial aspects of owning your own business.

5

Alternate Investment Theory

You have made it thus far! You are relatively certain that owning a business is what you want to do. To be absolutely sure that you are investing your money in the right place, it would be prudent to make a financial analysis of alternative investments. Look at some investments available to you and your family. It does not matter how uncertain the economic outlook is, your money should be invested in such a manner that you will achieve maximum return and safety on your investment.

What should you invest in? You may already be confused by conflicting advice from stockbrokers, real estate agents, precious metal merchants, financial columnists, and so on. Is it possible that all of this "advice" has done you more harm than good?

When it comes to investing your money, only you know the financial and personal factors that influence the kinds of investments that are suited to your particular situation. It is up to you to fit these factors into a program that best suits your needs. Then you can turn to the professionals for the final choice of investments.

RISK AND LIQUIDITY

Before you make any investments, you should reserve sufficient funds—apart from your business—to live on for at least six months. Your return on investments has many variables. In order to accurately gauge your return rate you must understand that the rate of return on any investment is a function of risk, liquidity, and tax considerations.

Some of the "danger" risks in investing are, for example, that oil wells can come in dry; an apartment, house, or motel may not be rented all the time. A company can go bankrupt and tax laws can change.

Understanding liquidity is very important. Money tax shelters must be held for a period of time before you begin receiving any cash distribution. In some cases you cannot sell your investment on a moment's notice, even in an emergency, without heavy penalties. The key to success is the proper combination of investments at the right time.

Is it worth the risk to start a new business? Are there alternative investments that will pay a higher rate of return than purchasing a business? When looking at your personal investments are they consistent with your long-term objectives? Review your alternative investments over the long term versus starting a new business.

To arrive at a reasonable estimate of the potential return, risk, and liquidity on your investment, first determine your total annual *family living* costs per month for the necessities of life: housing, food, clothing, utilities, car payments, insurance, debt payments, miscellaneous expenses, and all fixed and variable income. Then multiply this by six months. Your accumulated savings or current income or both should be enough, after providing for the above, to start you in your own business.

Once you have determined the amount you can prudently invest, the second consideration is—How liquid is your investment? Could you sell it right away and raise needed cash? Could you sell without loss of interest or penalty? Have you figured the cost of fees, commissions, and storage charges? Are you restricted to a specified time before you can sell? What rate of return do you want? What is your attitude toward risk and liquidity of the investment? Compare each investment very carefully. More and more investment plans are coming on the market—each has a specific purpose for the investor. The risks you are prepared to accept are by far the most important characteristic that distinguishes one investor from another.

Investments can manifest themselves in two objective ways: *loss* of capital and *loss* of return. How much can you afford to lose? Set limits that agree with your rate of return, risk, and liquidity. What is your primary reason for investing? Do you need income? Do you need capital gains tax treatment? Do you need deferred tax benefits? Set your investment goals and develop a program to meet your objectives.

DON'T SET YOUR SIGHTS TOO HIGH

It is not advisable to set your goals too high. In the five and a half years before the middle of 1979 the average annual rate of return (dividends plus price changes) for the thirty issues in the Dow Jones industrial stock index came to only 5 percent. Someone who had invested in high-grade bonds would have earned 5.9 percent during the same period of time. Figures that tell you that you can double your money in just a few years very often reflect "assumptions." It could, of course, be assumed that a person was very wise and bought at the very lowest figure and sold when the market reached its peak. The figures may leave out the costs of the transaction and the results may be computed for unrepresentative periods. It must be remembered that for the average person with limited assets, most of the avenues of investment are not practical or possible.

Compare some figures for the last one, ten, and fifteen years. The investments in the accompanying table are listed by percent of return. See how they have radically changed over the last fifteen years.

Using a scale of 1–10 (1 low–10 high) you can determine the risk and liquidity of other kinds of investments. For instance, a bank passbook has a low percent of return rate (5.25 percent) and very little risk (1). Most banks, credit unions, and savings and loan certificates carry $100,000 worth of state or federal deposit insurance, and very high (10) liquidity. You can obtain cash without penalty and loss of interest.

Inflation

Now consider inflation. 1986 was 3.8 percent. The last ten-year average was 4.5 percent; the last fifteen-year average was 6.9%. In 1980 it went as high as 18 percent. Bank passbook holders *lost* money as soon as they invested and continued to lose money as long as they kept their money in that type of account. The same was true for passbooks at savings and loans, treasury notes, common stock, Series E and H savings bonds, treasury bills, some Keogh retirement

Alternate Investments Theory

Compounded Annual Rate of Return as of 1985, Risk and Liquidity Investments

	Return Last Year	Return 10 Years	Return 15 Years	Risk (1–10)	Liquidity (1–10)
Foreign exchange	25.0	4.1	4.6	5	5
Preferred Stocks	20.6	0.4	0.4	4	8
Silver	39.8	9.7	10.3	4	3
Gold	29.1	9.2	11.9	4	8
Passbooks—banks	5.25	5.25	5.25	1	10
Passbooks—savings & loans	5.5	5.5	5.5	1	10
Treasury notes—long term (1 year)	5.7	5.7	5.7	1	8
INFLATION RATE	3.5	4.5	6.9	—	—
CONSUMER PRICE INDEX	3.8	6.5	6.9	—	—
Keogh retirement plans	8.0	8.0	8.0	2	1
IRA plans	8.0	8.0	8.0	2	1
Six-months money market (S & L)	8.3	8.3	8.3	1	9
Money market mutual funds	8.5	8.5	8.5	3	8
Series E Savings Bonds	9.3	9.3	9.3	1	8
Series H Savings Bonds	9.3	9.3	9.3	1	8
Treasury bills—short term (6 months)	5.7	10.2	9.2	1	9
Common stock	20.6	13.9	8.6	5	9
Corporate bonds	5.7	9.7	8.7	3	8
Rare books	9.5	9.5	9.5	8	2
Rare coins	14.5	15.1	18.2	4	5
Old Paintings (masters)	8.6	9.7	9.2	8	8
US farmland	−7.9	1.5	6.3	5	2
Single family homes	6.8	7.4	8.2	3	5
Apartments houses	9.5	9.5	9.5	4	6
2nd deed of trust	8.5	8.5	8.5	3	6
Real estate syndication	9.0	9.0	9.0	5	2
Commercial property	9.5	9.5	9.5	6	3
Oil	27.4	3.0	13.9	7	2
Diamonds	7.0	8.9	4.1	7	2
Commercial paper	10.0	10.0	10.0	5	7
US coins	10.7	16.3	18.8	4	2
Commodities	20.0	20.0	20.0	10	8
US Stamps	0.5	11.8	13.6	4	4
Chinese ceramics	6.7	11.3	8.3	7	4

Compounded Annual Rate of Return as of 1985, Risk and Liquidity Investments (continued)

	Return Last Year	Return 10 Years	Return 15 Years	Risk (1–10)	Liquidity (1–10)
BUSINESS OPPORTUNITIES					
Untrained owner	10.0	10.0	10.0	9	2
Trained owner	50.0	50.0	50.0	3	7

All opinions and estimates in this report constitute our judgement and are subject to change without notice. This report is for general information only and is not intended to offer or solicit purchase or sale of any security.

plans, IRA, IRA-rollover-tax deferred, and six-month money market certificates (savings and loan).

The small investor now realizes that the once-fashionable idea of saving for a rainy day is a considerable risk if inflation increases; and with the level of national debt, the poor balance of payments in international exchange, and the condition of the banking systems, the return of high inflation rates is a constant threat.

Bank Investments

Unfortunately, the national savings rate has dropped each year since 1975. Many believe that this spells trouble for the U.S. economy, because a lower savings rate always means a lower investment rate; consequently, a lower rate of growth and productivity. This in turn means that inflation can go even higher.

There are many theories on why we are saving less, the inflation is one of the most common. But it is also pointed out by economists that income tax laws tend to penalize savers and reward borrowers. As an example, interest earned on savings accounts is subject to federal and state income tax, while interest paid on home and property loans is tax deductible! Our tax laws, unfortunately, tend to encourage spending and discourage saving.

Real Estate Investments

Real estate is still widely perceived by most Americans to be one of the best investments. The return on a single family house is 6.8, 7.4 to 8.2 percent nationally.

Commerical property (9.5 percent), farmland (−7.9, 1.5 to 6.3 percent), and apartment houses (9.5 percent) did slightly better; but inflation went from 8.1 percent to a high in early 1980 of 18 percent, then settled down to 3.8, 4.5 percent in the mid 80s. The risk was moderate but liquidity became tougher as buyers could not qualify to purchase these investments. In considering inflation, realize that real estate is just a hedge and subject to a wide variety of conditions in the marketplace.

Solid Investments

Rare books (9.5 percent), old paintings—masters (8.6, 9.7 to 9.2 percent), oil (27.4, 3 to 13.9 percent), diamonds (7.0, 8.9 to 4.1 percent), U.S. coins (10.7, 16.3 to 18.8 percent), silver (39.8, 9.7 to 10.3 percent), gold (29.1, 9.2 to 11.9 percent), U.S. stamps (0.5, 11.8 to 13.6 percent), and Chinese ceramics (6.7, 11.3 to 8.3 percent) are investments with a higher percent of return, moderate risk, and more liquidity. All these items require a degree of expertise because they are very specialized investments. Now here is where you can start making money!

Some skeptics have decried the rising price of these specialized investments, stating that investors have "bid up" their prices to unrealistic levels. However, in 1980, most of these items outran inflation.

Those with excess capital are in a superior position. The literature shows that most people take a balanced approach to investments and will hedge their bets with "safe" investments such as bank or savings and loans deposit instruments. Remember, other people, events, and conditions decide these returns. Individuals have no control.

THE AMERICAN DREAM, OWNING YOUR OWN BUSINESS

Let us now look at the American Dream—owning your own business. So you want to achieve financial independence? Be your own boss? Business opportunities are where you have more control!

The economy has a great deal of control over your business but, over and above this, your success is determined by the business you select. How hard do you wish to work? How many hours are you willing to work? Do you want to run the business yourself or hire employees? In other words *it is all up to you*. The opportunities for men, women, and minorities are wide open.

By selecting the right business you can make inflation work for you. At least you can stay ahead of inflation and a recession. In other words, make the economy work for you.

Most people are of the opinion that many businesses fail due to poor management or lack of funds or both. In reality, people fail because they do not understand how to run their businesses. They do not ask enough questions to become truly knowledgeable about how the business operates and how it is financed. You need to get the answers from the previous owner, your own and the owner's accountants, an attorney, and a business broker. So the untrained business opportunity entrepreneur's percentage of return (10 percent) is more than inflation, and the risk (9) is higher because the business does not operate at its full potential. Liquidity is very low (2). The same business, with the owner trained by a professional organization such as American Business Consultants, Inc., in Sunnyvale, California, will have a higher percentage of return. It could go to 50 percent or higher with a more moderate risk (3) and higher liquidity (7).

Looking for a successful endeavor means starting out right, asking questions, learning the kind of business you want to know about, learning how to find that business, learning how to analyze financial records and books and how to finance a deal. You will also need to learn how to avoid common mistakes and pitfalls and how to avoid legal and tax consequences, how to use the proper contracts and agreements, and how to seek professional help. Once you have learned all these fine points you can then prepare a plan with reasonable goals. When this planning is complete your chances of making more money are realistic, and with the profit you make you can invest in a tax shelter or other tax-deferred plan.

TAX SHELTERS

Tax shelter investments should offer both investment merit and tax benefits. Monies paid to Uncle Sam can be used to purchase assets or income through tax deferral.

Understand that the amount of your tax shelter also depends on what federal tax bracket you are in. For example, if you are in the 28 percent tax bracket you generate a tax savings of up to 28 percent. Your situation will probably change each year. No two persons' situations are the same. This year's tax shelter need—maximum tax losses, maximum tax sheltered cash flow—will depend on your assets, liabilities, and lifestyle, plus your present and future income.

Unfortunately, under the 1986 tax laws, investment losses can no longer offset income from salaries, active business income, or even interest and dividend income.

There are hundreds of tax shelters within a business. If you need a car to operate your business, Uncle Sam does not say you must buy a Volkswagen or a Cadillac—it is your decision. There are also many tax considerations when you sell your business. If you plan to sell your business in order to buy another one you might be able to transfer your business assets tax free, such as tax deferred exchanges. We strongly suggest that you contact your attorney or your accountant or both to verify how the tax laws affect you.

Although the above examples are broad and generalized and subject to fluctuations in market value, interest rates, and tax law, they nevertheless will give you a general idea about the theory of alternative investment evaluation. It is important to establish personal guidelines for investment return, risk, and liquidity. Use these guidelines when making your decision about buying a business.

TRUST YOUR OWN JUDGMENT

When buying a business you *must trust your own judgment*. You can ask questions of well-informed professionals, but it would be unrealistic to expect them to be able to tell you something they do not know themselves; e.g., whether the stock market will go up or down tomorrow, or whether the property you purchased yesterday will be worth more tomorrow. Remember, most professionals know their own field, and however well-intentioned they are, they have a self-interest in trying to sell you their products or services for a fee. That is human nature!

You must make your own decisions. Don't get upset if you think you have made a wrong choice; everybody makes mistakes. Studies show that even the "experts" make errors, and sometimes an individual buying an investment like you are planning to do can make a better choice than an expert! Why? Because only you can decide what is best for you!

6

What Should I Pay for a Business?

It has never been easy to know what to pay for a business. The task seems burdensome and overwhelming. However, there is a reasonable approach—to subdivide the business, applying values to each area while keeping tax consequences in mind at all times. (See Chapter 14.) After you have studied your tax consequences, you will be ready to appraise your business.

BASIC PRINCIPLES

There are four basic factors of value for consideration when buying or selling a business:

1. *Utility:* This is based upon a business's highest and best use, or its usefulness. (This factor is a "subjective value.")

2. *Scarcity:* Short supply tends to increase the value of a business.

3. *Demand:* The larger the number of people seeking the same business, the more it tends to increase its value. This factor is implemented by those people having purchasing power.

4. *Transferability:* The possibility to legally convey title to a business.

APPRAISING A BUSINESS

One of the most difficult tasks in buying and selling Business Opportunities is appraising the business. There are three general methods of appraisal being used today:

a. Comparison (market value) approach

b. Cost approach

c. Income capitalization approach

Let us discuss each of these three methods:

Comparison (market value) approach   This approach is unacceptable in Business Opportunities. It requires that the appraiser find three or four recent sales of businesses similar in size and location. A difficult task at best! There are no two exactly alike, so beware. You can check the *McCords*, a daily publication, or multiple listing services at your local Real Estate Board for past sales. In an attempt to quantify the sales information gathered, there is a multiple regression analysis method which may be used to measure the relationship among three or more variables, such as selling price, location, size, and so forth. Due to the large number of variables, this approach can be very time consuming and the results questionable.

Cost approach   Cost approach is a disadvantage in Business Opportunities. Determine replacement cost, including the cost of all furniture, fixtures, equipment, leasehold improvements, inventory, liquor license, and so on, less depreciation. When real estate is part of the business calculate building replacement cost less depreciation plus land value. This method ignores subjective values such as location and goodwill, factors that carry significant value in Business Opportunities.

Gross Multipliers Are Worthless: Let's look at two identical businesses. Assume that everything is equal (i.e., gross profit and expenses) except rent. One business in a large shopping center has a very high rent, showing a loss on the business books. The other business, in a very low rent area, shows a good net profit on its books. Using the gross multiplier appraising technique, both businesses would be valued at the same price! Which one would be a better purchase?

Net Multipliers Are Next to Worthless: Let's again look at two businesses. A cocktail restaurant with $100,000 of "hard" assets, and an answering service with no "hard" assets. Both businesses produce the same net profit. Using the net multiplier appraisal technique, both would be valued at the same price! What happened to the value of "hard" assets?

Income capitalization approach   This approach is questionable in Business Opportunities.

Gross Income Less Operating Expense = Net Profit

Net Profit ÷ Capitalization Rate = Value

Income capitalization has been the most accurate method for comparing Business Opportunities *provided* expenses, net profit, and capitalization rate information has been derived from the same set of guidelines. This can *only* be determined by adjusting each business profit and loss statement before applying the capitalization rate formula. This method does not take factors such as goodwill, owner salary, depreciation, personal expenses, service debts, and so on into account.

New innovative appraising This is the "True Selling Price" approach. The only way to price a business is to establish a True Selling Price. (See the accompanying form.) The total value ("True Selling Price") of a business is based on the value of its assets plus the value of its "True Net Profit" or *ability* to make *money*. This ability is also known as "Goodwill."

Let's start out our business appraisal by determining what assets a business may have and how to determine the value of those assets. If you feel it is necessary, you may hire a professional appraiser to price out the business assets.

Asset Value

Asset value may be defined as the total value of equipment, fixtures, leases, franchise, and any other tangible items installed, less depreciation (i.e., market value). Assets may occasionally be referred to as "Hard Assets." Appraising the price of tangible items already in the business is *not difficult*, although it can be time consuming. List all the business property by category:

Accounts Receivable: Outstanding receivables must be "aged" to determine how old they are, if past due or current, and valued according to future income that may be expected. We always suggest that the buyer purchase these because the seller may apply too much pressure trying

---

Estimated Value of Assets

All assets (excluding goodwill)

Accounts receivable	$ _____
Inventory (at current wholesale cost)	$ _____
Work in progress	$ _____
Furniture, fixtures, and equipment (market value installed)	$ _____
Leasehold improvements (less used-up life)	$ _____
Lease value (residual and improvements, adjusted to market value)	$ _____
Franchise, trademarks, trade names, and formulas	$ _____
Logos, copyrights, patents, royalties, rights	$ _____
Licenses (ABC)	$ _____
Real property	$ _____
Customer lists number of accounts _____	$ _____
Customer contracts number of accounts _____	$ _____
Other assets (specify)	$ _____
Other assets (specify)	$ _____
Total asset value ("asset investment")	$ _____

---

to collect them after selling the business. The seller would have nothing to lose. You can use a similar approach such as that listed in the Lease Residual Value formula (page 76) to establish current market value.

Inventory and Work in Progress: These may be valued by determining current wholesale cost plus the percentages of work completed on the product.

Furniture, Fixtures, and Equipment: It should be clearly specified which assets are considered "trade fixtures" in that particular business. Some trade fixtures can become leasehold improvements, depending upon how they are installed, what the intent was of the business owner and the building owner, whether or not the fixtures can be removed from the premises without damage to the building or in restoring the building to its original condition, and *what the lease says*. (Read the section on leasehold improvements below.) What will the seller be taking away? What items are on loan or rented?

Identify each item. Some sellers "exchange" a business asset and replace it with a cheaper substitute. This may be deemed a fraudulent action. Determine the market value installed for each item. Market values may be determined by pricing a replacement item of similar age and condition, and adding installation costs. These values can be calculated using common sense. For example, what is the value of two-year-old tables and chairs, slightly scratched, with worn seats and shaky backs on some of the chairs? There are usually enough used furniture stores in town to determine today's market value. (See the yellow pages of your telephone book.) Use the same approach for used appliances. For specialty items call the manufacturer or distributor.

Trade fixtures are assets needed for the operation of the business. These assets are generally attached in some manner to the premises, but belong to the business owner and may be removed at the end of the lease period (if lease terms allow). An example would be, a sink installed in its own free-standing work counter. The sink is attached to the hot and cold supply system and to the drain system. Upon termination of the lease the sink and counter could be disconnected and removed by the business owner.

The sink with counter is a fixture. The water and drain lines are leasehold improvements. The appraised value would be the used replacement cost of the sink and counter *plus* the cost of the installation of hot and cold water lines *plus* drain line. Price the water and drain line cost as if you were doing an installation in an empty building where no water or drain lines are in existence.

Leasehold Improvements: Leasehold improvements are the toughest assets to deal with because of the way they are installed. The owner does not stop to think that some day the business will be sold, so the assets are installed as easily and as cheaply as possible; usually with nails, cement, or attached in such a way that the building owner can claim the asset as a permanent installation.

Sometimes a fixture is installed in such a manner that it becomes more costly to remove the fixture than it is worth. Leases generally specify that if you remove such improvements the premises must be restored to their "original condition." The building owner may do anything possible to claim the fixtures, although usually does not say anything while you are doing the installation. The building owner is delighted to have you improve the building; a good example is the installation of a large walk-in cooler which becomes part of the building in most cases. Should you wish to remove the sink we discussed earlier, and the building owner wants to keep it, he or she may try to insist that if you do remove the sink you must also remove the drain pipe—all the way to the street!

Another example is the installation of a large grill in a restaurant. The grill is permanently installed in place. In addition, the health department requires installation of an exhaust fan, hood, and vents. The fire department requires installation of an automatic fire extinguisher system. The total cost to the business owner for the grill system runs over $10,000, most of which is permanently installed and classified as leasehold improvements. Leasehold improvements *may* become the property of the building owners! Can the business owner sell something he or she does not own? The real question is—from a practical sense—could the business operate without the leasehold improvements? If the answer is no, then the improvement is part of the value of the business!

Leases: Many leases include verbiage similar to the following:

"Alterations: Without first obtaining Lessor's written consent, Lessee, its employees, agents, licensees, or contractors shall not (a) make or install any alterations, improvements, additions, or fixtures that affect the interior or exterior of the premises or affect any structural, mechanical, or electrical components of the premises, or (b) mark, paint, drill, or in any way deface any floors, walls, ceilings, partitions, or any wood, stone, or iron work. All alterations, improvements, additions, or fixtures, other than trade fixtures not permanently affixed to realty, that may be made or installed upon the premises by either of the parties, *shall be the property of the Lessor,* and, at the termination of the lease, shall remain upon and *be surrendered with the premises* as a part of the premises, without disturbance, molestation, or injury. Any floor covering that may be cemented or otherwise affixed to the floor of the premises shall be and become the property of Lessor."

In this particular lease, the business owner has given all leasehold improvements to the building owner "free of charge" at the termination of the lease.

Now, read this lease clause:

"Alterations: Lessee shall not make, or suffer to be made, any alterations, improvements or additions in, on, about or to the premises or any part thereof, without first submitting plans and specifications therefor, and obtaining the written consent of Lessor. As a condition to giving such consent Lessor may require that Lessee agree to remove any such alterations, improvements, or additions at the termination of this lease, and to restore the premises to their prior condition. Unless Lessor requires that Lessee remove any such alterations, improvements, or additions, any alterations, improvements, or additions to the premises, except movable furniture and trade fixtures not affixed to the premises, *shall become the property of Lessor upon installation* and shall remain upon and be surrendered with the premises at the termination of this lease. Without limiting the generality of the foregoing, all heating, lighting, electrical (including all wiring, conduit, outlets, drops, buss ducts, main and subpanels), air conditioning, partitioning, drapery, and carpet installations made by Lessee *regardless of how affixed* to the premises, together with all other additions, alterations, and improvements that have become an integral part of the building in which the premises are a part, shall be and become the property of the Lessor upon the installation thereof, and *shall not be deemed trade fixtures,* and shall remain upon and be *surrendered with the premises* at the termination of this lease.

"If, during the term hereof, any alteration, addition, or change of any sort through all or any portion of the premises is required by law, regulations, ordinance, or orders of any public agency, Lessee, at its sole cost and expense, shall promptly make the same."

In this lease the business owner *gives* all improvements to the building owner when *installed,* regardless how affixed to the premises. Trade fixtures shall not be called trade fixtures, but leasehold improvements. All the property shall be surrendered to the building owner at the termination of the lease. In these two leases you cannot sell something you do not own!

Although the business owner may not own the grill system, he or she does own the rights to use the system, over the *remaining term* of the lease. The business owner can sell leasehold *rights* as long as they are assignable. Now, the value of the grill system becomes part of the lease *value.* Lease value may have two components. Value of right to use leasehold improvements and value of lease residual.

Lease Residual Value: Occasionally a lease will have contractual terms wth an economic advantage if the lease, with the same terms, is assignable to the buyer. The economic advantage creates a *lease value.* The problem is, how does one assign a fair market value to a lease? (Note: It is possible to have a lease with detrimental terms, creating a negative value.)

To establish the value of the lease residual (see the accompanying case history on page 76) determine which lease terms have positive (or negative) attributes, compared to the terms of a new comparable lease that the building owner would be willing to issue for a comparable lease space. The most common value found in a lease would be a savings in monthly rent. The difference between the "economic" rent (today's market rent) and the "contract" rent over the remaining term of the lease is the basis of value.

To find the total savings from a given lease, multiply the remaining lease term (in months) by today's market rate, less the actual lease rate (per month, adjusted for any rent increase over the remaining term). The result equals the total savings due to the lease contractual terms over the remaining life of the lease.

Is the asset value of the lease equal to the total savings? No! A buyer will not and cannot be expected to pay this "savings" amount for the lease. Why? There is a "time value" to money that should be taken into consideration. The expected value of money saved in the future is affected by inflation and risk.

A ten-dollar savings in pocket today is worth ten dollars. That ten dollars can be used to purchase ten dollars of today's goods and services. Because of inflation, a ten-dollar savings in pocket five years from now will possibly only purchase five to six dollars of the equivalent of today's goods and services. In short, future dollars must be discounted back to today's values. Now, at what discount rate? We have already mentioned that the future value is affected by inflation and risk. The discount rate for inflation is based on your best estimate of expected inflation over the remaining life of the lease. The discount rate for risk is based on the terms of the lease and the longevity and profitability of the business. At best, risk discount is difficult to assess and is a value judgment. (Note: When the asset value of a lease is critical, contact an appraiser for a professional evaluation.)

The accompanying case history on page 76 will provide some insight in the evaluation of a lease asset.

Franchise, Trademarks, Trade Names, and Licenses: These asset values may be determined by market value comparison. Call the Franchiser or Alcohol Beverage Control Board and check to see what the current price is.

Real Property: Add the total value here, but handle real property (i.e., land and buildings) on a separate agreement form as an addendum to your purchase agreement. (Check with your local Real Estate Board.)

Case History: Lease Residual Value

Term of original lease in years:	20
Remaining life in years:	7.5
Economic rent (today's market value per month):	$ 1,116.00
Less contract lease (present) rent per month:	540.00
Savings per month:	$ 576.00
Savings per year: (× 12 months)	$ 6,912.00
Savings over remaining life of lease (7.5 years × $6,912 = savings per year):	$51,840.00
Calculate future value: $576/month savings for 7.5 years @ 8% interest average per annum savings account:	$70,717.91
Calculate present value: $70,717.91 discounted at 12% inflation rate + 6% risk rate (total 18%)	$20,506.89
Estimated value of lease:	$20,506.89

NOTE: Factors for future value and present value may be found in tables at your local library or bookstore.

Customer Lists and Customer Contracts: These asset values may be determined by analysis of future income that may be expected over the use of the contract or list life. Established future income should be discounted by inflation and risk factors to establish a current market value. (Use an approach similar to that used in lease valuation.)

Other Assets: Specify any other assets and their current fair market value, installed.

Financial Statements

We have looked at most of the intangible or "hard" assets you would expect to find in a business. Before we appraise the intangible asset value known as "Goodwill" we need to understand some things about how business owners "set up" their business records. To do this it is essential you have a basic understanding of financial records, books, and profit and loss statements. The business ability to make money is *supposedly* reflected in the business profit and loss statements. Many business owners "adjust" their sales and expenses to suit their own needs, manipulating them in different ways, both legally and illegally.

Some owners may "set up" the books to benefit themselves by showing different net profits for IRS, banks, and potential buyers of their businesses. The buyer must be alert to "discrepancies" in the books through discussions with the owner and observation of the business. Be sure to investigate the possibility of fraudulent business practices by the present owner.

A profit and loss statement in its purest form shows all the income a business has had and all the expenses it has incurred. If every business owner reported income and expenses by the same rules, evaluations and direct comparisons from one business to another could be made. However, they do not do this. Until you make a thorough investigation of a business for sale you do not know what the income and expenses amount to.

Business owners have conflicting profit and loss statement goals, reflecting the requirements of the owner. For example:

1. Tax purposes—maximum expenses and least profit;

2. Potential sale purposes—minimum expenses and maximum profit;

3. Covering up something;

4. Planning to use the profit and loss statement to acquire investors.

The question arises as to how *valuable* these reports are. It is very important to get at least a three-year pattern of profit or loss margins and also as much information on the business as possible in order to reconstruct the profit and loss statements which reflect the "real world."

In addition to a profit and loss statement (if not available, it can be created from scratch), ask the owner for the following:

a. Last three years of personal tax returns

b. 1040 Schedule "C" statement

c. Payroll tax returns

d. Personal property tax returns

e. Real property tax returns

f. Business books

g. Utility bills, etc.

h. Copy of lease

Talk to the business owner's banker, accountant, lawyer, suppliers, and if possible discreetly talk to customers. When evaluating the information gathered, look for: understated or overstated gross sales, overstated or understated expenses, personal expenses buried in the business, padded inventory, illegal deductions, and so on.

Balance sheet analysis   The balance sheet represents a "snapshot" look at the condition of a business as of the date of the audit only. It is normally made up by an accounting firm. Most Business Opportunities owners do not bother to have a balance sheet made up, unless the business is large or has been incorporated. If a balance sheet is available, various ratios may be checked to determine the condition of the business. Libraries, stock brokers, and accountants will have valuable information to help establish correct ratios for the type of business being reviewed.

The current ratio is the ratio of current assets (cash, marketable securities, receivables, and inventory) to current liabilities (all items payable within a year). Current ratio is a measure of a company's ability to meet its obligations over the next twelve months and still have ample funds to conduct its business effectively. Two to one (2:1) is considered a desirable minimum.

Another balance sheet item that deserves attention is "Book Value"; that is, total assets minus total liabilities (including preferred stock) divided by number of shares outstanding. A book value that is significantly higher than the market price of a company's stock is usually an indication that the company's assets are poorly managed.

Examine "Return on the Total Investment"; that is, net income divided by long-term liabilities and stockholders' equity.

If you are confused, we suggest that you take the advice of a competent accountant.

Adjusting the books Let's start to value goodwill by determining "True Net Profit." (See the form on p. 83.) True Net Profit may be defined as "True Gross Sales" less "True Business Expenses." True Business Expenses may be defined as all expenses *excluding*: amortization, debt service, equipment rental, depreciation, income tax, excess manager's salary, owner's salary, and personal expenses. All other expense is defined as "True Business Expense."

By adjusting the owner's stated net profit (by deleting the above excess expenses) you have in effect reconstructed the business profit and loss statement as if the buyers *paid cash* for the business and *operated* the business on a *cash basis*. This is the only way anyone can establish a useful basis of comparison from one business to another.

Perhaps the owner or the employees have been "skimming" from the business. Maybe the owner has inflated gross sales or net profit. It is surprising to know that most business owners will not attempt to inflate their gross sales because it increases taxes and often their rent (when a percentage lease exists). Seller's personal or nondeductible expenses may have been "buried" into business expenses. Ask yourself these questions:

Are the Owners or Employees or Both "Skimming" Cash from the Business?: Some examples are:

1. Jukeboxes, pool tables, and pinball and other vending machines provide a substantial amount of so-called nontraceable cash.

2. Service station gas pump prices may not match pump prices used in the books. A penny or two per gallon adds up.

3. Invoices that are not accounted for numerically provide opportunity for invoices and cash to disappear. A second set of dummy or extra invoices can accomplish the same thing.

4. Inventory may be sold for cash and not rung up on the cash register. The same can happen when a customer leaves cash on the counter and walks off, not waiting for a receipt.

5. An employee may accept a kickback or ring up a smaller sale amount than actual for the benefit of friends and relatives.

6. A bartender may "water" the drinks, or substitute bar inventory with personally owned bottles brought to work in a handbag or wrapped in a jacket perhaps, or brought in by an accomplice. The owner should count empty bottles.

7. The owner may "total out" the cash register a few hours before closing time, not reporting income for the balance of the day.

8. Owner or employee may issue credits for phony customer claims or returns, pocketing the cash.

9. Fictitious "accounts payable" can siphon business profits into someone's pocket.

10. An employee may "sell" copies of door keys or the combination to the safe to a friend for "mutual benefit."

11. Check dates on bank deposits. An owner should insist the manager make bank deposits on a daily basis. A manager may be taking money for personal use, hoping that the passing of time will cause confusion over what really happened.

Has the Owner Inflated Net Profit?: Inventory substitution and omission of hard-to-trace expenses can increase net profit shown on the business books. Examples:

1. Turkey as a substitute for chicken reduces food costs.

2. Cheap wine by the gallon can be used to refill more expensive wine bottles for resale in restaurants.

3. Inventory brought into Business No. 1 and sold, but charged to Business No. 2, reduces cost of goods sold for Business No. 1. Business No. 1 can then be sold at a higher price, based on its "higher" net profit.

4. Long-range pension plans may not show on books. Here is a liability to new buyer that can have far-reaching implications on long-term profitability.

5. Long-term notes on bond plan payments not on the books will also affect profits.

Are Personal or Nondeductible Expenses Being "Buried" into Business Expenses?: Some examples are:

1. Insurance ripoffs: Insurance expense may include personal auto, medical, life, or home insurance.

2. Utilities and telephone charges: Personal home or vacation cabin utilities or telephone charges may be deducted as business expenses.

3. Promotions and hidden expenses: Family outings, vacations, restaurant tabs, or alimony payments may be buried in promotional expenses.

4. Mortgage, rent, or lease cost: Personal home, vacation home, or friend's apartment costs may find their way into business rental expenses.

5. Payroll falsified: Payroll can be padded with family, friends, or phony employees. Terminated employees may be carried on the books beyond their termination date. Also, check owners unemployment tax rate. If it's high, this could mean a high turnover problem.

6. Equipment expenses: Personal automobile, boat, or airplane payments may be included in this category.

7. Inventory expenses: Personal food supplies and household items
   may be hidden as business inventory expense.

Actual Case Histories: A stock clerk for a shoe company parked his
car at the receiving dock. He kept his trunk closed but unlocked. At
12:30 p.m., when the shipping-receiving manager was at lunch, the
stock clerk threw full cartons of shoes into his trunk and then
slammed it locked. Elapsed time: eighteen seconds.

In another example, customers stood in line for one veteran sales-
woman. They refused to be served by anybody else. No wonder! She
switched tickets for many "special" customers, giving them substantial
markdowns. The store losses amounted to about $300 a week, not
including $25 a week in increased commissions for the crooked sales-
woman.

In another case where many returned items were marked down to a
fraction of their original cost due to damage, clerks got authorization
to buy "as is" merchandise. They then substituted their "as is" items
for first-grade items in stock!

Items in a thrift shop were ticketed in pencil. Some tickets were
unmarked. Since the store was inadequately staffed, many customers
marked down prices, switched tickets, or wrote their own prices.

A Word about Fraud: Fraud covers a broad spectrum of activity. It is
defined as gaining an unfair or dishonest advantage through deceit or
trickery. It covers outright stealing of merchandise, equipment, cash,
stamps, pencils, even rolls of toilet paper from restrooms.

As a final comment, some sellers will claim they are "skimming" from
their business to cover up an *inability* to make a profit. Never count on
sales or profit that cannot be verified!

True Net Profit

Now you are ready to "reconstruct" the profit and loss statement. (Use
the accompanying form, Estimated Annual "True Net Profit.") Using

---

Estimated Annual "True Net Profit" (Reconstructed)

Net profit (seller's books-12 months)	$ _____

Add backs (noncash, nonrecurring, excessive items and expenses buyer(s) may eliminate):

Depreciation	$ _____
Amortization	$ _____
Debt service (loan interest)	$ _____
Income tax	$ _____
Owner's salary	$ _____
Manager's salary	$ _____
Personal expenses	
Promotion	$ _____
Insurance	$ _____
Travel and entertainment	$ _____
Auto	$ _____
Other (specify)	$ _____
Expenses buyer may eliminate	
Equipment rental	$ _____
Discounts and refunds	$ _____
Bad debt	$ _____
Donations	$ _____
Extra employees (retiring)	$ _____
Other (specify)	$ _____
Income not reported (jukebox, pool table, games, etc., that may be verified)	$ _____
Other (specify)	$ _____
Add: Total adjustment =	$ _____
Total annual "True Net Profit" =	$ _____

---

the seller's profit and loss statement, transfer the annual net profit reported and add back the remaining values as stated by the seller as nonbusiness expenses as per our "True Net Profit" definition above. Forget "skimming." If you have knowledge of skimming you may be accused as an accessory to the crime. Now you have the "True Net Profit" of what the *business made*.

Risk Factor Scale: The "Risk Factor Scale" (below) equals a measure of how much *skill* and *training* is required for a buyer to take over *operation* of the business. This scale also measures the number of potential *buyers* available to purchase a business. The buyer should also consider the neighborhood, how long the business has been established, and the condition of the building.

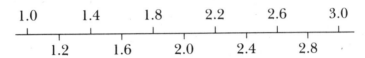

Skill:

| High | Average | Minimal |

Training:

| Years | Months | Weeks |

Types of Business:

Manufacturing	Retail stores	Sandwich shops
Scientific lab	Restaurants	Hot dog stands
Electronic plants	Liquor stores	Beer bars
Machine shops	Auto stores	Ice cream shop
Assembly plants	Bicycle stores	Hamburger stands
Medical lab	Variety stores	Billiard parlor
Engineering	Hardware stores	Snack bars

Buyers:

| Few | Most | Maximum |

Return of investment (Goodwill):

| 1 year | 2 years | 3 years |

We are now ready to establish the value of Goodwill.

Goodwill definition "Goodwill value" may be defined as annual "True Net Profit" less return on "asset investment," times a "risk factor."

First, consider that if the buyer did not purchase this business, he or she could leave the value of the "hard" assets in a bank and get at least

---

Estimated Value of "Goodwill" and "True Selling Price"

Annual "true net profit" (from
  page 87) $ _____
Deduct ____% annual
  interest earning rate on
  the total asset value "A" $ _____
Subtotal: $ _____
Goodwill Risk Factor ____
  (times subtotal) = $ _____
Goodwill (50% of Goodwill Risk
  Factor) = $ _____
Covenant Not To Compete: (50% of
  Goodwill Risk Factor) for ____ mile
  radius and for ____ years = $ _____
"True selling price" = value of assets, goodwill and
  Covenant Not To Compete $ _____

---

10 percent interest. Use an annual interest rate that would be considered a fair return on an investment. So the True Net Profit would be less valuable to the buyer and should be adjusted by subtracing this percentage return on the asset investment.

You then can multiply this sub-total by the appropriate "risk factor" to find "Goodwill Risk Factor."

Goodwill equals 50% of the Goodwill Risk Factor and the Covenant Not To Compete equals 50% of the Goodwill Risk Factor. 3 miles and 3 years is reasonable in most dense cities.

By adding the "Total Asset value," "Goodwill value" and "Covenant Not To Compete value" the result is the "True Selling Price."

Once the "The Selling Price" has been established, a business may be compared to every other business without distortion or confusion.

Buyer's "Net Spendable Cash" flow When comparing one business with another, there is one more major consideration to take into account. What is the buyer's "Net Spendable Cash" flow? Business

Estimated Annual "Net Spendable Cash" Flow		
Total annual "True Net Profit" (from page 87)		$_____
Less buyer's debts:		
Debt service payments	$_____	
Equipment rental payments	$_____	
New loan payments	$_____	
Other	$_____	
Total adjustments		− $_____
"Net Spendable Cash" to buyer		$_____

comparisons are made as if the business is bought for cash and operated for cash. In reality the buyer may not be able to eliminate some of the rental, lease, or financing costs of the business. Each business and each buyer's situation will be different. Reconstruct the annual "True Net Profit" to match your own situation.

For your convenience, the appraisal sections used throughout this chapter have been brought together on two forms: Estimated Annual "True Net Profit" and Estimated "True Selling Price." These appear on the next two pages. With a little practice you will become proficient in their use.

Buyer's tax and other considerations   If buyer and seller agree to a full replacement value on the furniture, fixtures, and equipment, the buyer will have a full (new) tax write-off, that is, highest possible depreciation.

If the buyer hires additional employees, he or she would get another 10 percent credit, plus the additional write-offs.

If you need unskilled workers you can get a tax credit of up to 20 percent off for each employee if you hire through the Federal Unemployment Office, WIN Program, in your local city.

In the past, there has been little said concerning tax allocation of the selling price. It boils down to being "tax wise." In most cases, "what is good for the buyer is bad for the seller, and what is good for the seller

Estimated Annual "True Net Profit"

Net profit (seller's books—12 months) $_____

Add back (noncash, nonrecurring,
excessive items and expenses
Buyer(s) may eliminate):

Depreciation	$_____
Amortization	$_____
Debt service (loan interest)	$_____
Income tax	$_____
Owner's salary	$_____
Manager's salary	$_____

Personal expenses

Promotion	$_____
Insurance	$_____
Travel and entertainment	$_____
Auto	$_____
Other (specify)	$_____

Expenses buyers may eliminate

Equipment rental	$_____
Discounts and refunds	$_____
Bad debt	$_____
Donations	$_____
Extra employees (retiring)	$_____
Other (specify)	$_____

Income not reported (jukebox,
pool table, games, etc., that
may be verified)(specify) $_____

Other (specify) $_____

Add: total adjustment $_____

Total annual "True Net Profit" $_____

Less buyer's debts:

Debt service payments	$_____
Equipment rental payments	$_____
New loan payment	$_____
Other (specify)	$_____

Less total adjustment $_____

"Net Spendable Cash" to new buyers $_____

NOTE: The above information has been supplied by the seller from his books and financial records.

Estimated "True Selling Price"

All assets (excluding Goodwill)

Accounts receivable*	$ _____
Inventory (at current wholesale cost)*	$ _____
Work in process*	$ _____
Furniture, fixtures, and equipment (market value installed)	$ _____
Leasehold improvements (minus used-up life)	$ _____
Logos, copyrights, patents, royalties, rights	$ _____
Lease value (residual and improvements, adjusted to market value)	$ _____
Franchise, trademarks, trade names and formulas	$ _____
License(s) (ABC) others _____	$ _____
Real property	$ _____
Customer lists number of accounts _____	$ _____
Customer contracts number of accounts _____	$ _____
Other assets (specify)	$ _____
Other assets (specify)	$ _____
Total asset value ("Asset Investment")	$ _____

Goodwill

Annual "true net profit" (from page 87)	$ _____
Deduct _____% annual interest earning rate on the total asset value "A" $ _____	
Subtotal:	$ _____
Goodwill Risk Factor _____ (times subtotal) =	$ _____
Goodwill (50% of Goodwill Risk Factor) =	$ _____
Covenant Not To Compete: (50% of Goodwill Risk Factor) for _____ mile radius and for _____ years =	$ _____
"True selling price" = value of assets, goodwill and Covenant Not To Compete**	$ _____

*Any variations between estimated and actual values of any of these three items shall give Buyer(s) the option of paying: ☐ cash ☐ increase/decrease the number of monthly payments on Buyer(s) note to Seller(s) ☐ new note to the Seller(s)

**The total selling price of the business is less any outstanding liabilities, such as: liens, encumbrances (notes) etc. The above information has been supplied by the seller from his books and financial records. The broker, or its agent(s) has reviewed these books and financial records. Broker, or its agent(s) do not warrant the accuracy of the information contined herein.

is bad for the buyer." However, in reality, the "allocation" of the selling price is determined by "hard facts," *the cost of the business assets plus Goodwill.* In essence, you have completed most of the "allocation" when you valued the business. There is very little to negotiate. The valuation of business assets provides the basic information for allocation, although some of the values are subjective and may be reasonably negotiated between buyer and seller.

Covenant not to compete   This is part of the "Goodwill value" you determined in estimating the "True Selling Price." To value the covenant not to compete, first look at the seller: Is the seller young and in good health? Has the seller indicated any future plans to stay in the area? If yes, the value could be set *high.* On the other hand, is the seller ready to retire? Moving out of state? Found another business (not related to the one you are buying)? Is the seller sick and unable to work any more? The value in the latter cases could be set *low.* You can use a similar approach, as used in the Lease Residual Value formula above, to establish current market value of the "covenant not to compete." This value should be subtracted from the Goodwill value established for allocation purposes. The total "Allocation" has to equal the total "True Selling Price."

7

How to
Finance a
Business

There are various ways to purchase a business with little or no money down:

1. Look for a business about to go bankrupt in which the owner wishes to get out from under.

2. Offer to take over all debts of the business if the owner will sell you the business with "no money down." Some owners will be happy to get rid of their headaches and will go along with the idea.

3. Hire a good appraiser or accountant to evaluate the value of the inventory and equipment in the business. Look for a business that has a lot of assets in relation to its debt, and borrow against those assets.

4. Buy the business with "no money down."

5. Contact all the business creditors and refinance the debts for as long as possible. Try for a reduced settlement.

6. Sell off as much equipment as possible, keeping just enough to permit the successful operation of the business. Collect old bills. Attract new markets for your products by streamlining the operation. You may make a profit within a short time.

"Instant business success" stories often tell about taking over a going business with little or no cash down. This appears on the surface to be the best way to buy a business. The fact, often not mentioned, is that the buyer is wealthy and puts up suitable collateral (assets) at least equal in value to the loan balance owed against the business. If the buyer has a large amount of net worth there is a better chance that a seller will consider taking a lower down payment and carry back a note for the balance of the purchase price. The stronger a buyer appears to be financially the more readily other creditors, note holders, and equipment lease holders will allow the buyer to assume notes or extend credit.

If a thorough study, as outlined in this book, is made of a prospective business there can be a cash flow from the first day of operation. This immediate cash flow should cover loan obligations.

Let's look at several major sources and techniques that, alone or in combination, are available for financing a new business.

SELLER'S FINANCE

Sources

1. Seller financing can be a marvelous investment opportunity. Many sellers do not need all of the cash out of the sale of their business. Carrying some or even all of the financing for the buyer and the business can be a very wise investment for the seller. A considerable amount of financing can be done simply by assuming the seller's existing debts, such as loans on the business, fixtures and equipment loans, and lease or lease-back agreements.

2. If the buyer is short of cash, consider as a down payment some personal property no longer needed; for example, boats, automobiles, furniture, motorcycles, recreational vehicles, stock, or bonds. Maybe a seller would like to have what the buyer does not want! Look over the seller's balance sheet: Can you purchase any outstanding notes at a discount? Return any inventory to tower the selling price? One never knows until a purchase offer is made.

Buyer's Advantages

Immediate response: Buyer can usually negotiate more satisfactory terms and conditions with a seller than with a financial institution.

Buyer's Disadvantages

There are relatively few, if you follow instructions given in this book.

Seller's Advantages

1. Quick release of obligations, especially if the seller is moving or there is a divorce or death in the family.

2. Seller financing is one of the safest investment opportunities available to the seller today because it is secured by what the seller knows best—his or her own business.

3. Business owners will most likely sell their businesses faster.

Seller's Disadvantages

1. Seller may lose extra interest charges otherwise carried on other notes or in another investment.

2. The buyer may sell off and ruin the business, or walk away from the business leaving the seller with a note secured by a useless asset.

LEASE A BUSINESS WITH OPTION TO BUY

Although it is not a common occurrence, a seller of a business may consider leasing the business when buyers with cash are hard to come by. Here is a good opportunity for a novice buyer to obtain a business without spending a large sum of money and taking on unnecessary obligations. The buyer puts up first and last month's rent and a security deposit. The total deposit is applied toward an agreed-upon purchase price when the option is exercised, usually in one or two years.

The lease payments cover the seller's obligations and give the seller a return on his or her investment. There may be an "excess" to the lease fee which may be applied to the purchase price of the business.

Buyer's Advantages

1. Low amount of cash required.

2. There is low risk.

Buyer's Disadvantages

1. There is no ownership.

2. Buyer may not be able to meet the terms of the option.

3. Buyer may lose the deposit.

4. Buyer may have to give up a successful business.

Seller's Advantages

1. More buyers are able to meet the terms.

2. There is a monthly income.

Seller's Disadvantages

1. There is no release from current and possibly future obligations incurred by the business.

2. Buyer may ruin an existing business and walk away with little to lose.

3. Seller's cash is tied up in the business.

PERSONAL LOANS

Sources

1. Banks, savings and loans, insurance companies, credit unions, finance companies, and other "private" lenders. These sources tend to fluctuate with the economy.

2. Buyer may rely on immediate family or friends. The cash value of a life insurance policy is an excellent cheap source of cash down payment. Insurance policy loans are at record levels today due to the low cost, usually 5 percent or 6 percent for such borrowing. In the event of the policyholder's death the loan proceeds are subtracted from the policy payment to the beneficiary.

3. Some sellers and lenders will finance close to 80 percent of a sale if the buyer gets a wealthy co-signer to make a personal guarantee. Employers sometimes are willing to co-sign for key employees. One overlooked loan source is existing employees.

4. Borrow the down payment. Thousands of credit-worthy buyers borrow their cash down payment. Although the repayment terms may be stiff because most loans are unsecured signature loans, the sacrifice may be worth being able to buy a business at today's prices rather than delay and pay a higher price in the future.

5. A loan that would offer a low interest rate would be one secured by personal assets, such as an automobile, mobile home, boat, airplane, stock, bonds, and equipment loans, against insurance policies or other tangible assets. The higher the risk, the higher the interest rate will be. It is difficult to get a bank to carry notes just

against a business. In most cases a bank will ask for additional security. Their feeling is that in reality there are little or no "hard" assets with marketable value in most small to medium businesses.

6. Subject to certain restrictions, savings customers are able to borrow against their savings accounts. The maximum loan is generally 80 percent of the account balance, and the interest rate is 2 percent over the interest rate paid on certificate accounts or 1 percent over the interest rate paid on passbook accounts.

7. Real estate loans are the most common source for money needed to purchase a business. Here are some ideas: When the buyer owns real estate, perhaps some vacant land or income property, that property can be offered in trade as down payment on a business. If the buyer does not want to dispose of current property, then a second or third mortgage may be created against that property and the mortgage note offered as a down payment on the business. The cost of creating and recording such a mortgage on property already owned is about $10 and carries a relatively low interest rate.

8. Many buyers forget that in most cases real estate equity loans have a maximum loan limit of 80 percent. If you own a house worth $100,000 with $20,000 equity, as far as financing institutions are concerned you have *no equity* to borrow against. You cannot count on the 20 percent equity for a down payment on a business or for anything else.

Buyer's Advantages

1. Possibly there will be more liberal credit terms, which can help in starting out with a new business.

2. Buyer may structure lower monthly payments and lower interest rates on created notes.

3. Buyer retains the benefits of appreciation of property mortgaged.

4. Buyer benefits from maximum leverage of money invested in both real property and a business.

5. This is a more rapid method of raising capital than some other sources.

Buyer's Disadvantages

1. When borrowing from a relative, there is always the possibility that the relative could hamper business operations.

2. There is a high probability of strong reaction to nonpayment or slow payment on secured loans. If a buyer defaults, he or she will not only lose the business but additional assets as well.

Seller's Advantages

1. Seller can assist in qualifying buyer for business purchase.

2. There can be tax benefits. (See a tax consultant.)

3. Seller is protected when other assets are used to secure notes. (Consult an attorney.)

Seller's Disadvantages

1. There may be problems after the sale but before the transaction can close, from buyer's relatives' interference or family disagreements.

2. Seller's equity used leaves no cash available for new ventures.

3. Outside loan sources may take some time to approve buyers. Also they may require most of the collateral, leaving the seller holding a note without much security.

ACCOUNTS RECEIVABLE, FACTORING VERSUS LOANS: THE MAJOR DIFFERENCES

"Factor" is a factoring organization that *buys* all well-rated accounts receivable, some purchase orders, invoices, contracts, secured loans, and notes for immediate cash. For any uncollectables, the factor absorbs the loss; the borrower does not incur any obligation.

In a commercial finance company "loan," the borrower *assigns* his or her accounts receivable as collateral for a *loan* and remains responsible for any uncollectable debt. This is called "with recourse" and is the usual method employed.

The accounts receivable may be financed through commercial financing companies on a "notification," where the customer is informed of the assignment and is asked to remit directly to the lender. "Non-notification" means the payments are made directly to the borrower by the customer, and in effect the customer is not aware that the borrower has assigned his or her accounts receivable. This method does not disturb the borrower's relationship with the customer.

The effective rate of interest compares quite favorably to an unsecured bank loan wherein a discount is deducted in advance and wherein the bank insists on maintenance of a compensating bank balance of up to 20 percent of the loan amount. The main consideration is not the cost but what goals can be accomplished using this financing method as compared to not using it.

Commercial factoring organizations have greater experience in credit and collection information and generally have larger financial resources than the average business. They bridge the gap when a borrower cannot meet the cash requirements from retained earnings or unsecured bank credit and the sale of equity is neither feasible nor desirable. Lenders, before granting a loan or purchasing accounts receivable, will evaluate management's capabilities and offer advisory services to help set up a sound operational policy. These methods may improve your tax position. Consult your tax accountant or attorney for further information.

Factoring

Here is how factoring works. ("Company" refers to factoring organization.)

1. The Company purchases your accounts receivable net of current invoicing less a one-time discount.

2. There is no reserve.

3. There is no recourse pertaining to credit on original invoices mailed.

4. The Company may handle all collection in business name, thus speeding accounts receivable retirement.

5. A monthly aging report is submitted to your business as a permanent accounting record.

6. There is no charge for invoice mailing or postage.

7. The Company has credit checking available on new clients.

8. New applications are approved and funded generally within two working days.

9. There is usually no minimum. Your business determines how much and how often.

There are several innovative factoring techniques developed to fit varying credit needs of a business.

Maturity Factoring

Borrower receives payment from lender on the receivables on the average maturity date of monthly credit sales.

Export Factoring

This is basically the same as above, except lender specializes in *export* shipments. This guarantee of payment serves to allay the fears of businesses about the political and credit risk involved in foreign trade.

Cost of commissions, credit, collections, and protection against credit losses varies (¾ percent to 1½ percent of net sales, plus interest charges of 6¾ percent to 8¾ percent—in mid-1980). These charges vary from account to account.

Accounts Receivable Loans

The borrower *assigns* 100 percent of his or her accounts receivable and may borrow up to 80 percent of accounts assigned to the lender as the security for the cash advance. When the borrower collects the accounts receivable, the cash value is given to the lender to reduce the borrower's indebtedness. This is a continuing arrangement and the originally retained deposit is refunded.

Banks and commercial finance companies do not consider themselves to be money-lending agencies but rather providers of revolving working capital. Charges from commercial finance companies will vary with the prime rate, usually 3–5 percent over prime rate. Commercial banks charge prime rate plus 1 percent to 3 percent, plus a service charge which varies. This charge may be based on carrying a compensating balance or a fixed amount per invoice or a percentage of the average monthly loan balance.

Buyer's Advantages

Cash flow: If there are sufficient accounts receivable outstanding, the buyer may elect to turn them into cash and use the cash as a down payment, as working capital, or for expansion. This would have to be spelled out in the purchase (deposit receipt) agreement. This method would give added leverage and flexibility during negotiations of the sale of a business.

Buyer's Disadvantages

If seller, bank, or finance company are overly aggressive, they may use undue pressure in collecting, and may cause possible alienation of customers. The customers may refuse to buy any more products from the new business owner.

Seller's Advantages

1. Seller can sell the business quicker.
2. Seller can protect and improve credit rating.
3. Seller can improve cash up front.
4. Seller can borrow needed working capital without losing control of the business.
5. Seller can turn all or part of accounts receivable into immediate cash on a flexible basis, as fast as seller can ship merchandise to meet day-to-day operating overheads.

6. Seller can improve business credit standing and can better project sales and operations by (a) improving facilities, equipment, and advertising; (b) paying bills on time; (c) taking advantage of cash discounts; (d) taking advantage of any profitable opportunity, acquisition, expansion, or temporary reversal; (e) receiving cash to finance next season's production (otherwise seller might have to close down business until the funds come in); (f) increasing volume by carrying more and larger receivables; (g) helping a business balance sheet look better by improving the current ratio and debt/equity ratio; (h) avoiding the need for a partner; (i) devoting full time to profit-making ideas rather than worrying over money problems.

Seller's Disadvantages and Limiting Factors

1. Most commercial financing companies are interested in companies that have annual sales over $250,000, or extraordinary growth in manufacturing, or that are converters or that are jobbers.

2. Lenders are usually not interested in a consumer service business or retail business. Lenders will only finance certain customers based on *their* paying records.

3. Seller will have to age and discount accounts receivable.

VENTURE CAPITAL

Sources

Individuals or firms that specialize in either debt or equity loans for start-ups, expansion, turn-arounds, acquisitions, and inventions.

Buyer's Advantages

It may enable a non-credit-worthy experienced operator an opportunity to operate a business with competent financial assistance for a percentage share of the business, or obtain a loan at a higher rate of interest.

Buyer's Disadvantages

A buyer may have to give up a considerable percentage of the business, or operate with an unknown management team which may make unreasonable demands. Buyer may also have to make other concessions.

Seller's Advantages

It may enable seller to complete transaction with a buyer who might not qualify otherwise. Seller can sell a highly specialized business when other lending sources are not available.

Seller's Disadvantages

Venture capital specialists often take a long time to approve a project and may make considerable demands for information.

GOVERNMENT LOANS

Sources

There are possibly over fifty different government agencies ranging from the well-known national agencies (SBA, EDA) to little-known local and regional agencies. (A mention of government grants in this section is appropriate. Such grants are available to a large range of businesses, with wide diversification. However, these are not loans and they have entirely different terms and conditions.) It is wise to seek the assistance of qualified professionals for these types of loans. Unfortunately, it is not possible to go into all the possibilities. However, we will discuss some of the better-known government agencies that assist with business loans.

SBA Loans

The Small Business Administration is an excellent source for financial counseling and reference materials.

There are two basic types of SBA loans:

Bank loan guarantee programs These are bank loans which the SBA will guarantee up to 90 percent to the bank for qualified applicants with 25 percent to 30 percent equity. Once the bank approves the loan, its terms and conditions, the SBA will usually notify lender of guarantee within thirty days. Funding takes a couple of weeks. Total turn-around time is forty-five to ninety days.

Banks are normally acquainted with the SBA requirements. (Some banks are not well versed in, or do not want to participate in, SBA loans.)

Interest rates for SBA Guaranteed Loans range from ½ percent to 2¾ percent over prime rate, depending on whether it is a long- or a short-term loan. There is often a bank charge of 1 percent of the loan amount as a loan origination fee. Average length of loans range from five to fifteen years. Credit requirements are somewhat less stringent than usual lender requirements.

Direct loans   Much less money is loaned under this program than under the Bank Guarantee Program. Interest rates range from 2 percent to 3 percent to 8½ percent to 14 percent, depending on the program. Lowest rates go to handicapped and disaster-type loans. Loan ceiling is usually $100K. Several programs are listed below:

Minority

Handicapped

Solar/Energy

Viet Nam veteran

Women in business (Limit–$20K)

Government contracts (usually Bank Loan Guarantee)

Construction (usually Bank Loan Guarantee)

Import/Export (usually Bank Loan Guarantee)

Credit requirements are often quite liberal; usually only 20 percent to 30 percent equity in the business is required. Qualifying for unusual features can often be a real boom to a small business. Applications are complex and turn-around times are generally six months or longer. SBA requires the maximum collateral possible on direct loans. Professional assistance is definitely recommended if you do not want a turn-down. Two to three bank turn-downs are required for most applications to qualify for a direct loan.

Buyer's Advantages

It may enable buyer to qualify for either a larger loan than would normally be possible (Bank Guarantee Program); or it will allow buyer to borrow *some* money when none is otherwise available.

Buyer's Disadvantages

Buyer may lose a business which he or she wishes to purchase while waiting for a SBA Direct Loan because of loan turn-around time; approximately 15 percent of total loans can be used for working capital. This may cause a financial hardship when a considerable amount of working capital is required.

Seller's Advantages

It may allow seller to sell to a wider range of buyers. It also enables seller to cash out if desired.

Seller's Disadvantages

Most sellers will not wait for SBA funding. It can take six to nine months before the buyer is able to obtain funds. There is no assurance of funding until SBA approves the loan and funding date.

For situations that make a business ineligible for a SBA loan, see the information on p. 106, courtesy of SBA Management Aids No. 170.

Note: Reconstruction loans and some disaster loans have rates as low as 2 percent to 3 percent but are usually limited in scope and are somewhat difficult to obtain. Then there are VA loans for businesses that have low down payments and interest rates.

Situations That Make a Business Ineligible for a SBA Loan

The Small Business Administration cannot lend money in the following situations:

- If the company can get money on reasonable terms:

  (1) From a financial institution.
  (2) By selling assets which it does not need in order to grow.
  (3) From the owner using, without undue personal hardship, personal credit or resources of partners or principal stockholders.
  (4) By selling a portion of ownership in the company through a public offering or a private placing of its securities.
  (5) From other government agencies which provide credit specifically for the applicant's type of business or for the purpose of the required financing.
  (6) From other known sources of credit.

- If the direct or indirect purpose or result of granting a loan would be to:

  (1) Pay off a creditor or creditors of the applicant who are inadequately secured and in a position to sustain a loss.
  (2) Provide funds for distribution or payment to the owner, partners, or shareholders.
  (3) Replenish working capital funds previously used to pay the owner, partners, or shareholders.

- If the applicant's purpose in applying for a loan is to effect a change in ownership of the business; however, under certain circumstances, loans may be authorized for this purpose, if the result would be to aid in the sound development of a small business or to keep it in operation.

- If the loan would provide or free funds for speculation in any kind of property, real or personal, tangible or intangible.

- If the applicant is a charitable organization, social agency, society, or other nonprofit enterprise; however, a loan may be considered for a cooperative if it carries on a business activity and the purpose of the activity is to obtain financial benefit for its members in the operation of their otherwise eligible small business concerns.

- If the purpose of the loan is to finance the construction, acquisition, conversion, or operation of recreational or amusement facilities, unless the facilities contribute to the health or general well-being of the public.

- If the applicant is a newspaper, magazine, radio broadcasting or television broadcasting company, or similar enterprise.

- If any of the gross income of the applicant (or any of its principal owners) is derived from gambling activities.

- If the loan is to provide funds to an enterprise primarily engaged in the business of lending or investments or to provide funds to any otherwise eligible enterprise for the purpose of financing investments not related to or essential to the enterprise.

- If the purpose of the loan is to finance the acquisition, construction, improvement, or operation of real property that is, or is to be, held primarily for sale or investment.

- If the effect of granting of the financial assistance will be to encourage monopoly or will be inconsistent with the accepted standards of the American system of free competitive enterprise.

- If the loan would be used to relocate a business for other than sound business purposes.

LEASING

Sources

Banks, insurance companies, manufacturers, distributors, suppliers, leasing companies, sellers.

This method of financing is usually beneficial to only those companies that would prefer not to tie up too much cash capital. The advantages are:

1. Lower down payment;

2. Generally lower payments than amortized loans;

3. Payments often can be tailored to suit one's pocketbook;

4. Lease payments are tax deductible directly, whereas loan payments are not.

The disadvantages are:

1. Loss of ownership (cannot be included in assets);

2. Higher qualification requirements;

3. Higher insurance costs;

4. Loss of sales tax deduction and depreciation;

5. There is usually no ownership at the end of the lease period without a surcharge.

Some of the types of leasing for depreciable equipment are:

1. *Small Equipment:* Office equipment, tools, etc.

2. *Fixed Equipment:* Large machinery, manufacturing equipment racks, etc.

3. *Rolling Stock:* Vehicles used in transport of various types.

4. *Autos/Boats/Planes:* Personalized business-use vehicles.

5. *Business or Expansion:* Loan money for an investment based on the equity of the business. (See Bank Loan Guarantee Programs above.)

6. *Sale/Lease-Back:* Article is sold to lender and leased back. (Note: Sale/lease-backs can be used for virtually any assets.)

A lender will often lend against the entire building or business. A note of caution regarding leasing: *Watch out for the IRS on leases.* It is a good idea to check on what is deductible and what is not on a lease arrangement. Often the IRS in an audit will call a lease a purchase contract. Questionable lease items include paintings, antiques, art of various types, and so on. If the lease period is less than the depreciation schedule allowed by the IRS, or if there is an unusual use or application, the taxpayer should be prepared to defend (and perhaps lose) his or her tax position. Some lenders will "pass through" the tax credits to lessor on some leases. Investigate the IRS tax position on these lease terms also.

Buyer's Advantages

Buyer will not have to tie up much capital to acquire use, and can report the lease cost as an operation expense with no liability to show on a balance sheet. There are usually better benefits than depreciation.

Buyer's Disadvantages

It cannot be used as an asset on financial statements.

Lessor's Advantages

Seller retains title to equipment and tax write-off benefits (if needed to offset sale income).

Lessor's Disadvantages

Repossession can sometimes be difficult; equipment salvage value may not pay off indebtedness.

INVENTORY LOANS

Sources

Sources include suppliers, distributors, manufacturers, and commercial finance companies. There are different ways that merchandise can be obtained:

1. *Trade Credit:* This represents a major source of funds. Suppliers will often extend credit for goods purchased, and usually grant a 2 percent discount from payments made within ten days. Or, a merchant may take thirty days to pay without discount.

2. *Consignment:* Merchandise can sometimes be delivered, if requested, on consignment. That is, suppliers retain ownership of inventory, receiving payment when inventory is sold.

3. *Warehouse Receipts:* Merchandise occasionally can be delivered to a warehouse or stockroom, even one located on the business property. This provides a "free" supply of inventory for the merchant to draw from immediately and pay for as it is used.

4. *Billing:* Suppliers can be asked to ship inventory now and bill in ten to ninety days. A few suppliers, will on request, extend credit terms up to 120 days.

5. *Cash on Delivery (COD):* This is often required on new accounts from suppliers, or the merchant may wish to pay on delivery.

6. *Seasonal Dating:* Suppliers will often send "seasonally dated" goods well before a particular season starts. Payment is not due until the season is underway. Monthly billing can be established if requested by the merchant.

7. *Unsecured/Secured Loans:* These are used when a merchant pledges all or part of the inventory as security to the supplier. This will assure a dependable source of supplies and bind a merchant and the supplier together.

8. *Floor Planning:* This type of flooring financing is done through banks and commercial finance companies. They will finance up to 80 percent of the merchandise value. It works like this: The lender stocks up the showroom or store. The merchant pays the lender as the goods are sold. This "loan" is a form of consignment and is called a "revolving account." Title remains with the lender until sold, but merchant has possession and agrees to keep merchandising in trust for the lender. This form of financing is usually used for large items such as automobiles, motorcycles, boats, home appliances, and so on. Ten percent to 18 percent is usually charged on the outstanding balance calculated at a daily interest rate.

9. *Credit Cards:* This is a form of a loan from suppliers and banks.

FREE EQUIPMENT

It is quite common to get vending machines such as pool tables, video games, pinball equipment, and so on *free* and also receive about 50 percent out of sales receipts. Some vending equipment dealers will loan up to $3,000 on a beer bar and $6,000 on a cocktail lounge with very low or no interest charges, just to get their equipment into your business establishment.

Suppliers and distributors often supply free equipment if you purchase supplies from them. This is a good way to get coffee makers, coolers, freezers, dispensers, and so on. Sometimes a building owner will purchase equipment for a tenant and add a little more money to the monthly rent to cover the equipment cost.

CREDIT LINE

This is usually an informal understanding between a businessperson and a bank or supplier to grant loans on a combination of a multitude of personal and "hard" assets for short-term funds for a maximum amount agreed upon at any one time.

CUSTOMER'S ADVANCES

This means advance payment against orders for future production and delivery. It is used mostly on high-priced items with long deliveries (one-third with order, one-third when shipped, and one-third when delivered).

GO PUBLIC

This means sell stock in your own company. See an investment house about this method of raising money. (Note: *Be careful* if you are forming a "closed" or nonpublic corporation and intend to sell stock to raise capital. A NASD license is necessary for this type of sale if it is sold to ten or more persons. This can be a useful method of raising capital but can be dangerous if done incorrectly.

CASH

A business can always be purchased for cash. Incidentally, this is a "naughty word" in business. Most sellers and buyers, after they have studied the tax consequences and their financial resources, will not accept or offer all cash.

8

Negotiations

When dealing with sellers, building owners, noteholders, lessors, creditors, and franchisors, negotiations require a lot of preparation and presentation. When the right answers to potential questions are presented in a straightforward manner the battle is half won. The remainder is a matter of adjusting terms (needs) in a reasonable way fair to all parties involved.

First, review all terms and all conditions of leases, notes, and contracts. Check to see if the language, "will not unreasonably withhold consent to the assignment," is included in the terms of the document; otherwise you must get this commitment from the lessors and assignors.

Second, contact each lessor/assignor whose consent will be required for an assignment of lease, note, or contract to the buyer:

1. Establish a relationship of effective communication, confidence, and trust with lessors/assignors.

2. Obtain from each party a commitment to assign, extend, or rewrite the lease, note, or contract. Determine revisions to existing conditions, terms, new applications required, or other demands.

PREPARATION

Lessors/assignors are looking for a person with a good credit rating, experience in the business, business plans, and ability to repay. The following package should be prepared in advance of negotiations. It should contain most of the information required when negotiating with any of the parties in the transaction. (Make sure that there are enough copies of each document for each party involved before negotiation proceedings commence.)

1. A purchase (deposit/receipt) agreement

2. A buyer's financial statement

3. A buyer's resumé

4. A buyer's authorization agreement

5. A letter of intent

6. A lessor/assignor application

7. Assignment forms

THE SELLER

The seller's attitude toward a buyer will be based (in most cases) on how strong the buyer is financially. The seller wants a buyer who is able to run the business satisfactorily. A well-prepared resumé and financial statement will create a good impression with the seller. The buyer wants the seller to accept the purchase offer and financing terms. When a positive impression can be created in the mind of the seller there is less reason for concern about the buyer's business abilities and the risk involved in carrying back financing.

If the buyer signs the "promise not to disclose information" form (see page 118), it will put the seller more at ease. The seller will then be more willing to show books, records, and operating information to the potential buyer.

BUILDING OWNERS, NOTEHOLDERS, LESSORS, CREDITORS, AND FRANCHISORS

Each of these persons has goals and motives. Try to analyze the position of each before making an appointment for a presentation. Generally their goal is to increase money in their pockets. There may be motivation for increase in security, potential long-term gain, property improvement, improved payment schedule, or an increase in business.

THE APPROACH

The approach to each of these parties is very important. Have the following applications filled out: Assignment forms, Purchase (deposit/receipt) Agreement, and a Prospectus of Intent (see page 119).

The prospectus of intent should include the following information:

1. Redecoration plans

2. Items to be repaired, replaced, etc.

3. New equipment purchase plans

4. Changes to be made in product or service or both

5. Time schedule and budget information to accomplish intended plans

6. Advertising plans

7. Growth projections of gross sales

8. Management and organization plans

A well-thought-out business plan will show each party the buyer's strength and positive direction. The potential buyer is asking the building owner, noteholder, lessors, creditors, and franchisors to invest in the buyer's ability. They need good reasons to believe the buyer—a stranger—who is taking over obligations from a seller they already know. Do not give them any reason to say *no*, just reasons to say *yes*!

PROMISE NOT TO DISCLOSE

I promise not to discuss or disclose to any third party that the business specified below, may be for sale, exchange or transfer, or otherwise disposed of. Further agree not to disclose any facts learned about the business to any third parties, including employees, customers, vendors, other prospective buyers. The information and/or records about this business obtained by me shall not be used for competitive use in any business, present or future. I understand that information disclosed to others could cause a loss of business, and/or create injury to employer–employee relationships. Should any legal action be taken against me as a result of this agreement, the prevailing party shall be entitled to court costs and attorneys fees as awarded by the courts.

To:_____
      Seller's name

_____
      Seller's business name

_____
      Seller's address

X _____ Date _____ , 19___ .
      Buyer

_____
      Print name and title

X _____ Date _____ , 19___ .
      Buyer

_____
      Print name and title

_____
      Buyer's address

SAMPLE LETTER: PROSPECTUS OF BUSINESS INTENT

_____

_____

_____ 19___

_____

_____

_____

Dear Sir:

As prospective owners of _____ located at _____ , we propose to implement several changes for the purpose of increasing the gross sales of the business.

My wife/husband and I will be involved in the operation and management of this business.

Several physical improvements, repairs, replacements are anticipated as follows:

The interior will be redecorated in Spanish decor, adding new tile, wall paint, carpets, pictures, and light fixtures. Repairs will be made to the kitchen sink and a new stove will be installed to improve kitchen thru-put time. The men's room wall tile will be replaced. We have budgeted $30,000 to accomplish these improvements.

Within four months from takeover of the business, we will have a "Grand Opening," supported by a substantial advertising campaign with 10,000 announcement flyers which will be distributed in conjunction with six months of heavy newspaper advertisement. We believe in substantial budget allocation for a continuing advertisement program.

We project that the improvements, serving Spanish food and with Spanish decor, supported by advertising and good management, will increase our gross sales by 40% within the year, and will greatly enhance the attraction of your shopping center.

Very truly yours,

_____

Buyer

_____

9

Operating My New Business

Congratulations on owning your own business! Now, let's make it work!

Taking over any business is difficult until the nuisances and quirks of the operation are familiar. During your training period, don't attempt radical changes. Take time to analyze the reasons the previous owner set up the business to operate the way it does. Changing the operation of a business should be a slow, thoughtful, evolutionary process. Remember your customers. You may alienate them by too much change too soon.

The welfare of your employees and the goodwill you wish to extend to customers should not be outweighed by tedious procedures. Because your business grows and expands should not mean overgrown paperwork. Often business managers run their businesses from crisis to crisis. They had not planned clear procedures; consequently, their businesses run them. They become pencil and paper pushers, tediously plotting out the use of money, materials, and manpower. The result is minimum efficiency, unhappy employees, and disgruntled customers.

TWELVE WAYS TO CUT DOWN EXPENSES

There are many ways to cut down on expenses especially if you have just taken over an established business. Study the twelve ideas given below:

1. Look at your product. Do you do your own packaging? If so, can it be sold unpacked or with less expensive wrapping?

2. What about cheaper products for your restroom? Try buying them in bulk or on sale.

3. If your employees make too many personal telephone calls, tell them they will be charged so much per call. This wastes too much company time.

4. If you have employees ask them for ideas on how to cut down time spent doing certain jobs. See that staff do not waste too much paper, pencils, notepads, and other office supplies.

5. Offer some kind of incentive, such as a day off with pay, for a "saving idea."

6. Get machines overhauled before they break down. It's cheaper than buying new machines. Be sure to include maintenance costs in your operating budget.

7. Can you do with less office or storage space? If so, ask the building owner if you can sublet, thus saving rent for yourself, and perhaps make a small profit on your lease.

8. What about travel expenses? Can salespersons use the phone or write letters? Using these facilities saves the wear and tear on an automobile and the sales budget.

9. Ask customers if they would carry their own packages, or make small delivery charge if goods have to be delivered outside, say, a ten-mile radius of your store. Or just make a flat delivery charge for all deliveries.

10. Form letters eliminate employing a secretary. A typist can easily fill in this type of letter. Cut down on salaries this way.

11. To reduce maintenance and cleaning charges, paint the lower half of your office walls a darker color.

12. If more than one letter is going to the same person the same day enclose all in one envelope. Make sure that your postage meter is accurate. Get the post office to check it.

EXTERNAL POLICY

Your external policy should be molded as your reputation becomes known in the community. Until you build a reputable relationship with each of these parties, there will be quite naturally some suspicion directed toward you the new owner on the part of building owners, suppliers, and creditors. Be friendly, straightforward, and pay debts on time. A good relationship will be established quickly.

Then you can start to change external policy. You can then seek better terms, larger discounts, more business, more credit, new contracts, and promotional considerations. Map out your goals. Show the other party their advantages in dealing with you, then entice them to go along with your requests. Don't forget! A strong relationship is a must if you expect cooperation.

INTERNAL POLICY

Finally, because the people who work for you are crucial to the success or failure of your business, it is important to establish a solid employee policy. Employees are fearful of new owners. They do not know what you expect or whether or not they will be treated fairly. Be *firm* but *fair*. This is the only policy that will work. Establish rules quickly and enforce them firmly and fairly. You will be respected as the boss and will gain maximum efficiency from your employees.

Nevertheless, you want your business to operate smoothly and to prosper. Analyze all major areas of your business for efficiency of operation. Start scrutinizing internal problems. They are crucial to operating efficiency and the control of your business. Don't let red tape overrun the more basic need for adequate business controls. Simplify as much as possible the paperwork required to get the job done and to make the business operate smoothly.

Operating Procedures

Planning changes is the key! First analyze the existing system. This is best accomplished by writing down every action it takes to complete a task. Use a large blackboard or roll of paper. Beginning in the upper left-hand section, write down your procedure, moving from left to right. When you reach the right-hand edge, move down a section and begin from the left again. One well-defined task may have hundreds of steps, but you will understand how that task is accomplished. The use of planning symbols will simplify the effort and make the disclosure more readily readable. Second, analyze each procedural step. Determine which steps cause wasted effort and may be eliminated or combined. Using this method you will also see holes in your control system. Add any steps necessary to fill the gaps; add steps necessary to improve efficiency.

Up to this point, everything has been on paper. Your third action in planning changes is implementation. If possible, this should be done section by section. This will minimize disruption of your business and any negative reaction from your employees. Remember, changes to an operating system are easier to accomplish when well thought out on the blackboard or on paper. Your employees will appreciate a well-planned approach and can often add meaningful suggestions. They will be less resistant to change in procedures when they have been included in the planning process. Written operating procedures should be created for the following areas:

Cash receipts	Purchasing
Receivables	Inventory
Payables	Work in process
Payroll	Manufacturing

Fourth, analyze each document used in the business. This action works hand in hand with the development of task procedures. Once each task has been defined, document format will fall into place.

As you develop operating procedures as outlined above, here are some things to keep in mind.

You will want to know as much as possible about the people you hire to operate your business. Start with a comprehensive employment application. Although it may seem bothersome, keep a separate file folder on each employee. Write notes on your good and bad impressions about employees and actions you observe while they work. File your notes in their folder. These notes will help you decide about pay raises and future promotions.

Maintain a good set of financial records. Many business owners fail to keep adequate records which are necessary for operating the business and for filing with the IRS. Set up clear, concise, itemized daily budget controls by area, department, and product lines. Know your volume of sales versus controllable and noncontrollable fixed and variable expenses. Your business decisions will be made based on knowing the financial picture of your business. Budget controls should include the following:

Record register readings three times per shift.

Record use of discount coupons daily.

Record employee meals daily.

Record credit card sales daily.

Deposit cash in bank daily.

Keep daily payroll time records.

Maintain detailed inventory records by area or department, quantity and price.

Purchasing inventory and supplies   Here is an area greatly abused in many small businesses. It takes quite a bit of experience to optimize the purchase of inventory and supplies needed in your business. You will need to learn what quantities and what quality products to purchase, buying enough to keep your customers happy with the selection, yet keeping inventory turnover at a reasonably high level so your invested dollar is earning maximum return. Buying too much inventory is good for your customers, but can be disastrous to the small business. High inventory levels mean risk of obsolescence and/or spoilage. If your product requires refrigeration, buy only what will fit your unit.

A Word about Computers

The small business computer has come into a price range that cannot be ignored by the business owner. Computers with the capabilities of systems costing hundreds of thousands of dollars a decade ago, are now available in the $2,000 to $15,000 price range—in some applications, less!

Computers are used in business to complete routine repetitive tasks, which can be time consuming, or to compile valuable information which might be ignored because of the time required to process the data. Here are some uses of computers in business.

Accounting:
  Payroll   Accounts receivable
  General ledger   Accounts payable
  Budget planning   Tax returns
  Financial reports

Marketing:
  Sales forecasts   Sales budget planning
  Marketing proposals

Purchasing:
  Purchase order control

Manufacturing:
  Product control   Inventory control
  Material requirements
    planning

Clerical:
  Mailing lists   Form letters
  Standard contracts   Customers' contracts

These are a few of the uses for a computer system. A computer is not a substitute for a business owner or an accountant, but is rather a powerful adjunct for the successful business person. The system must be used and controlled to be effective. This will take some of your time. If you are not willing to learn how to use your computer effectively, to spend time using the system, and to have the computer become part of you, don't buy one!

10

Making
My New
Business Grow

You have selected and purchased a business with which you are now familiar, operating in much the same manner as did the previous owner. Now it's time to grow—which means more sales, customers, and sales per customer.

Growth can be accomplished if you have a plan. Redefining the needs of old and new customers; letting them know you are ready and able to fill their needs is very important. To accomplish this you need to attract old, new, and potential customers through advertising, personal contacts, promotional efforts, additional services or products, and by contacting old customers with better offers of new services and products.

CHECK YOUR COMPETITION

Check your competition carefully. Your product should be sold at competitive prices and quality, and must of necessity be a little better than your competition who is selling similar products. Estimate the number of competitors who are likely to spoil your chances of success in or around your area. Find out why your competitor's product sells more frequently than yours. If necessary buy a quantity of your competitor's similar items and compare them with your quality and selling price. Do a lot of "shopping around" before you buy new product lines for your business.

MARKET PLAN

Another point to watch: Is there a need for another product of similar nature in your chosen area? How do you propose to market your product—through wholesalers or direct to the consumer?

Marketing can be defined as finding out what people will buy and what they will not buy from you or anybody else, then getting them to buy from you!

There is no point in spending hundreds of dollars on a scientific research project to find out whether or not your potential business will pay. A simpler way is to set up a questionnaire, make it as short and as concise as possible, and ask your present and potential customers to tell you what problems they have encountered with a particular product if any. Ascertain the reasons why they will or will not purchase the article from you. The questionnaire should include questions like: When you entered my place of business was the service good or bad? Did the assistants help you find what you were looking for? Did the product hold up? What new services or products would you like me to offer so that your shopping is made easier by purchasing what you require from my place of business?

Because you are a small concern, you can tailor your business to meet your customers' needs much better than a larger operation can because your business is more personal and friendly. Larger businesses do not have time to be friendly or to discuss products with their customers. Their overhead is higher, and perhaps the manager is watching the hired help to make sure they don't spend too much time with one customer and as a consequence lose another! Therefore, as a small business owner, study and analyze your own specific market and focus on a target that fits your own capabilities. Then you will find that your business will succeed because you have taken the time and trouble to determine and fulfill the needs of your customers.

A small business owner has only limited resources to spend on marketing activities, and must concentrate on promoting existing products before expanding horizons and marketing new products.

According to SBA 89 there are four key marketing decision areas in a marketing program: "(1) Products and services, (2) Promotion, (3) Distribution, and (4) Pricing." This is a good "mix."

Products and Services

This area should include concentrating on one item at a time, developing it, and then selling it.

Promotion

Promotion includes advertising, selling skills, and similar activities. One must have good quality salespeople in a small business to make it successful. Good advertising is a must; although expensive, it should be part of every budget. There are different ways to advertise a product—through the mail, in the Yellow Pages, or in the daily newspapers. Flyers can be printed and distributed. Coupons can be attached to ads and contests can be held with prizes or reduced prices for certain items.

Remember, most businesses are "neighborhood businesses," deriving profits from customers in the local area. After obtaining new customers, don't let your advertising dollar go to waste! Develop a customer list and maintain contact with each one through direct mail. The frequency of contact will be determined by the average life of the service or product offered by your business. As your business grows, there will be a greater need for innovative advertising campaigns.

A variety of advertising media are available to get your message across to the customer. However, choose your media carefully. The wrong choice, message, or timing can cripple your campaign and budget and ruin your growth potential. Reaching a potential market may appear simple, but in reality it may be far more complex. The business world is very competitive, and even though you *think* you are familiar with certain aspects of a business, a wrong message can spell failure. Careful planning, commitment, and experimentation are necessary for optimum results in any advertising program.

Distribution

This depends on your product and your potential market. If you are a manufacturer who ships to a wholesaler, who in turn sells to a retailer who sells to a consumer, the markup will be higher than if you as manufacturer sell directly to the consumer. This again brings up the question of location, which is so important when buying or setting up a business. The nearer your business location to your potential buyer, the more cheaply your product can be sold. If you have large transportation fees to pay, the product will have to be sold at a higher price.

Pricing

The higher the price often means fewer sales, but this of course depends upon your product, especially if you are promoting one item at a time. If servicing an item is included in the price it will naturally make the cost higher than if it were sold outright with no after-sale service. This is something a new owner has to take into consideration in a marketing campaign.

After you have completed your market survey of your customers, review the questionnaires to ascertain what will be needed to improve your business. It is important that you do all you can to make yourself customer-oriented and ascertain from time to time how your employees treat your customers, making sure they are satisfied with their purchases and will return to your store.

The U.S. government has many publications available for small businesses. Some are free and some cost a small fee. (For a list of these publications see Appendix II.)

GROWTH PLAN

The secret to growth is attracting and keeping customers!

All your policies should be aimed at giving entire satisfaction to your customers. The profit made per item is much more important than sales volume. According to the SBA 89 pamphlet, "To use the marketing concept . . . " a small business should:

1. Determine the needs of its customers (see "Distribution" above regarding questionnaires);
2. Analyze its competitive advantages (a small business can tailor its services to customers better than larger competitors);
3. Select specific markets to serve (try to serve the local community before expanding into new territories); and
4. Determine how to satisfy the needs of the market at hand.

Add new products and services slowly, and key your cash register to determine the effects of new inventory. Also key old services or products to determine whether or not to keep them.

11

Do I Want
to Sell
My Business?

By this time you should be reasonably well informed. You have searched for and purchased a business. You have gained control, developed your business, and made it grow. This has naturally increased its value. Now it is time to move on to a greater challenge! A new horizon!

Before you decide to sell, there are some questions that you should ask yourself. A truthful evaluation of yourself and your business will go a long way toward confirming your decision to sell and your real reasons for doing so. Answer the following questions to see if you are ready to sell your business. Check the appropriate box:

	Yes	No
Do I work reasonable hours?	☐	☐
Do I have time for a 2-week vacation?	☐	☐
Are my financial rewards adequate?	☐	☐
Can I replace myself?	☐	☐
Am I in control of my business?	☐	☐
Can I further expand my business?	☐	☐
Have I built a good customer base?	☐	☐
Have I built a good service product line?	☐	☐
Can I take the day to day stress?	☐	☐
Do I get along well with employees and customers?	☐	☐
Do I have new competition?	☐	☐
Has there been a major change in my family's needs?	☐	☐
Is my business financially healthy?	☐	☐
Have I really made the business grow?	☐	☐
Do I have enough capital to continue growing?	☐	☐
Can I handle two businesses?	☐	☐
Do I have to move?	☐	☐

	Yes	No
Do I have any medical problems?	☐	☐
Can I make any improvements?		
Fix up inside or outside of building?	☐	☐
Replace furniture or fixtures?	☐	☐
Replace machinery or equipment?	☐	☐
Change employees?	☐	☐
Change or add product line/service?	☐	☐
Move to larger quarters?	☐	☐
Other _____	☐	☐

Answer the questions honestly. The answers will provide insight into your motivation to sell or not to sell and more than likely will give you some ideas about the problem areas in your company. The problem areas can then be dealt with before you attempt to sell your business. Honesty in evaluating your business will help you when you sell it.

The formula and method for selling your business is the same as it was for purchasing it (review Chapters 1 through 8), but now look at the business through the eyes of a seller. Just reverse the questions and answers. Determine whether or not it is ready to be sold.

Make sure that all your business records are up to date. Have a profit and loss statement, balance sheet, any other financial statements available for inspection, and a copy of your lease—to aid the potential buyer to ascertain the "True Net Profit" and to demonstrate how you arrived at the "True Selling Price." (See Chapter 6.)

CHECK OUT POTENTIAL BUYERS

It is important to check out potential buyers and find out if they have sufficient capital and background knowledge to make the business a success. When checking into the finances of buyers do not sign any papers until you are certain they have sufficient financial resources to handle the transaction. (Very few people are willing to risk all of their own personal capital in a business.) By doing so, you will not be wasting your time with people who have insufficient funds and little or no experience operating your particular kind of business. These people are not likely to buy any business and are wasting your time. (See Chapter 15.) You may ask, "Why worry about who buys my business; I want out." An unqualified buyer may create problems for you by running the business into the ground and losing all your customers; as a consequence the business may have to close down. If you have taken a note on the sale of the business you will be left with an unpaid debt and may wind up with the same business, but in a very bad condition! Your building owner, note holder, franchisor, and creditors will want to know how financially strong your buyer is before they will do business with that person.

YOUR REASONS FOR SELLING

You must be truthful about why you are selling the business. Many buyers will rely on your reasons.

If you are really sick and not just sick of the business spell it out—heart trouble, pending operation, allergies to products, death in the family. If you are moving for health or for any other reason tell the potential buyer where, when, and why. If the reason is financial, make it clear to the buyer: divorce; partnership breaking up; cannot make it; had a better offer to return to industry; want to purchase a larger business or another type of business. Answers should be ready for any type of question that may be asked. Be very honest; do not make lame excuses about why you want to sell; and please *stick to your story!*

YOUR REAL ESTATE BROKER

If you need help in selling your business, it is wise to contact an attorney, an accountant, and a real estate broker before you offer it on the market. A good reputable broker who will screen potential applicants before presenting them to you can be of great help. Of course, if you sell through a broker, there is generally a fee of 10 percent. This fee is negotiable and not fixed by law.

Brokers will ask for any one of three different types of listings:

1. *Exclusive Listing:* That is, regardless of who sells the business, including yourself, the broker will receive full commission.

2. *Agency Listing:* That is, if any broker sells the business the exclusive broker will receive full commission, but if you sell it, you will not owe a commission.

3. *Open Listing:* That is, whoever sells the business receives the commission—you may have any number of brokers to whom you may wish to give a listing. If you sell it yourself, you don't have to pay anyone.

This relieves you of all the "Looky Lous"—however, make sure the broker is a business broker who is capable of selling a business like yours. Select one who has experience selling similar businesses and is familiar with your business and methods of analysis (especially if you own a specialty business).

A good business broker can bring to you a buyer who is ready, willing, and able to buy a business. A good broker is able to help you make decisions on things like price, terms, financing takeover, and evaluating offers and help you through escrow (see Chapter 19).

Note: Before you decide to sell, lease, lease with an option to purchase, lease/back, or create a partnership, do not fail to investigate all of the tax consequences of selling your business. You may consider exchanging your business for a "like" business (tax deferred exchange). Bear in mind that exchanges are very complicated and should not be attempted without a competent professional tax attorney and/or tax accountant.

This evaluation will help you decide where the greatest potential lies for you. Read this book completely before you make your final decision.

12

What Is My Business Worth?

The seller see things differently than the buyer does.

As the seller, look at the transaction through the eyes of the buyer who also wants a good return on his or her capital. The buyer must be able to earn a living from the business since presumably this will be the sole source of income. In most cases the buyer is buying a job. If the business is not going to be profitable, no sensible buyer will buy it. No sensible buyer will buy a low-profit concern, unless it was neglected through poor management, low financing, ill health, death, divorce, partnership breaking up, and so on. If you must close your business before it can be sold, you may still have a chance to sell your hard assets, furniture, fixtures, and equipment at market value installed, although you will not receive anything for goodwill. A buyer is normally a very shrewd person, like you were when you purchased the business. Therefore, look at the buyer's point of view just as you looked at your own when you purchased this business.

You (the seller) have had to put a lot of money into the business and natually want to get a return on your capital outlay.

Don't expect the buyer to pay for any mistakes you may have made in running the business, nor pay for any furniture or equipment you replaced because of poor judgment. That would be unreasonable and unfair to the buyer. Future earning power is the thing that the buyer is looking for, not making up for your past failures and inability to work as well as you should have or wanted to. Blood, sweat, tears, and investment are for naught if your business is unhealthy.

VALUE YOUR BUSINESS HONESTLY

The value of your business is based on hard assets and *past* excess net profit rewards. The growth in value of your business is related to the growth in net income you created or took advantage of while you owned and operated that business.

The formula for what to expect a buyer to pay for your business is the same as the one you used to purchase that business (see Chapter 6).

PRICE YOUR BUSINESS REALISTICALLY

Be sure to price your business realistically or it will never sell. When potential buyers feel the business is overpriced they are less inclined to make an offer, even though they may be interested in purchasing it.

What the new buyer intends to do with the business is really of no concern to you unless he or she purchases it on an installment plan; that is, the buyer remits to you a certain sum of money each month. In cases like this you are better off employing a real estate broker who is qualified in the sale of businesses. The broker will make sure the buyer is a responsible and qualified person.

REFRAIN FROM PROJECTING PROFITS

When a potential buyer seems interested in purchasing your business, do not attempt to project what profit it might make. You do not know the buyer and you have no idea what the buyer's future plans may be. Let the buyer make his or her own projections. The buyer may decide from a personal point of view that the business is so profitable there is plenty of time to play golf and neglect the customers, who consequently go elsewhere to buy the merchandise. Or the buyer may turn to you the seller and say "If it's all that easy, why don't you do it yourself?" However, looking at the sale more logically, the buyer may make changes that will affect the operation, product, employees, and so on. The buyer may lose all your old customers, thereby making all your projections invalid and leave you with a possible law suit for misrepresentation.

Remember, a seller wants to get top price and the buyer wants to pay the lowest price possible. This is human nature; and if all the facts are presented and the seller is straightforward about the business, there is no reason why a sale should not go smoothly, resulting in both a satisfied buyer and a satisfied seller. The most important point! *Be prepared.* Have everything completely ready, as prescribed in this book. The buyer will detect it if you fumble or fail to answer his or her questions. The buyer may lose interest and you may never know why.

13

How Should
I Finance
the Sale?

"I want all cash!" This is the universal demand of sellers. In doing so they alienate and eliminate most potential buyers, except the 5 percent who can pay all cash.

But the all-cash buyers are few; most buyers won't be able to discuss the purchase of a business by cash even though they qualify in every other respect. For example, a buyer with $50,000 can buy a business worth that amount. But what's the point? A buyer with $50,000 could put it all down on a one-half million dollar business! A buyer with cash does not have to settle for a smaller business. It would be unwise to do so, because the buyer wants a maximum amount of income leverage.

In most cases then the seller will get a lower sales price for the business. When buyers *offer* all cash, in most cases they offer 25 to 30 percent *less* than the asking price and usually settle for 15 to 20 percent less. The result is that the seller will pay more taxes! Yes, more! If you insist on an all-cash sale, you will pay a higher percentage of tax in the year of the sale. With proper planning, you can reduce your tax rate and pay tax over several years rather than in one large lump sum (see Chapter 14).

CASH VERSUS INSTALLMENT SALE

For example, let's compare a cash sale versus an installment sale in which the buyer can offer all cash. Of course, 95 percent of the buyers will not offer all cash, but if they do, the seller ends up with 15 to 20 percent less than the asking price. Also, the seller has to pay the entire tax, which might be substantial, in the selling year.

The seller must be aware of the tax and legal consequences at the time of sale, as well as for future situations. The seller should carefully consider using an installment sale in order to prolong the tax payments over several years. The installment sale will allow more potential buyers with limited resources to put less cash down. It will also allow the seller to carry the balance and increase the sale proceeds from the additional interest charges. In reality then you can get *more* than the asking price over the longer period.

Consequently, the seller can generally get the full asking price by taking less cash and by paying income taxes over the life of the note. The seller can in fact enjoy a steady income. For example, if the seller's loan to the buyer is $50,000 at 10 percent interest over 7.2 years, interest-only payments, the seller would double his or her money during that period. The seller would receive $100,000 ($50,000 in principal plus $50,000 in interest) plus the 15 to 20 percent savings for getting full price for the business.

OTHER SOURCES

There are, of course, other sources of finance for business. The seller may take a personal loan from a relative, a friend, a bank, an insurance company, a credit union, a finance company, or a private lender; or may obtain a government loan, an inventory loan, or a line of credit from a bank or a supplier. The seller then transfers the loan to the buyer at escrow closing (see Chapter 7). Most sources, however, are highly dependent on the buyer and his or her business strengths, in addition to other security the buyer may be able to offer the lender or supplier.

BUYER TO ASSUME

Are there any encumbrances (notes) which may be assumed or transferred? Are there any furniture, machinery, or equipment notes or leases to assume? Anything the buyer can assume will probably have a lower interest charge than today's high interest rates. Assumed notes and leases will reduce the amount of cash needed to buy the business.

TRADE

Barter is the world's oldest form of exchange. If a buyer is short on cash, consider accepting a boat, automobile, motorcycle, recreational vehicle, furniture, jewelry, stocks, or bonds as a down payment. The possibilities are almost endless.

There is a case where the buyer offered labor to build an extension onto the seller's house in trade for the down payment on the seller's business. In another case, the buyer sold the seller's accounts receivable and used the cash for the down payment (see page 100).

Now! A new twist to trading—cowboy auctions. The auction is based on the original barter concept for business people who can trade their services, products, or equity in personal items like autos, houses, jewelry, boats, airplanes, antiques, and so on. The auction board looks like an organization chart, with bidder A at the top. Bidders B, C, and D bid for A's bid, and so on.

A has offered art valued at $10,000 at the top of the board. B has offered a '78 corvette, C has offered a two bedroom home, equity value, and D has offered a painting contract, all valued at $10,000

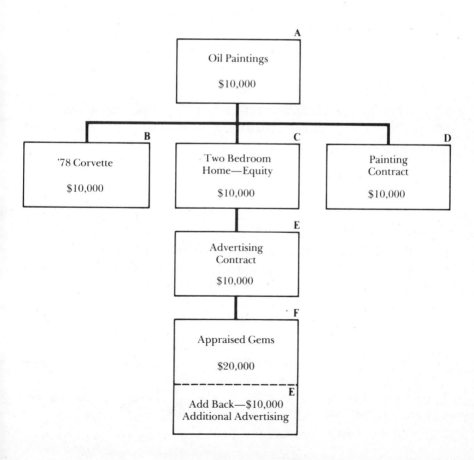

each, for A's $10,000 of art. E doesn't like A's art, B's corvette, or D's painting contract; E has offered $10,000 of advertising on C's $10,000 home. F, on the other hand, wants E's advertising and F knows E is in that business and can double F's bid, so F offers $20,000 in appraised gems for $20,000 of E's advertising. Now, A has the choice of the board, and, let's say, accepts B's bid. Now, C can accept E's bid and E can take F's bid. This goes on and sometimes as many as twenty bids appear on one board. Let's look at another example.

To get a little more creative, you have a $100,000 business; you trade for a $100,000 ranch to retire on, or a yacht, or another business. It also works if you only have, say, $20,000 equity in the ranch. What if the buyer doesn't have the exact equity amount to exchange for the service or item you wish to exchange? The buyer or seller can add something else; for example: the seller is trading equity of a $100,000 business, a $50,000 home, a $5,000 boat, and a $10,000 trailer, totaling $165,000. Now the buyer can offer for all or any part of the trade package something that the seller wants, say a $105,000 airplane and a $50,000 note.

Now, when money is tight and cash is becoming passé, with the introduction of credit cards, bartering is sweeping the country and becoming a new way of life.

RISK

As far as risk goes, the seller should insist that the buyer put the business up as security only if the seller has a buy-back clause; that is, if either the gross sales or the inventory falls below 75 percent in a given time period the seller can repossess the business. Risk to the seller is minimal, especially if he or she has additional security. If the seller, for instance, has sufficient funds to purchase all or part of the equipment and lease it to the buyer, risk will be reduced.

In the final analysis, as a business owner, you will obtain the most satisfactory results if you are willing to finance the sale of your business yourself. When the sale is structured properly, you can trade for that retirement ranch, you will have immediate use of it for yourself and your family, you will pay less tax, receive a monthly income, and have minimum risk exposure.

14

Tax
Advantages

Through consultation with your CPA or attorney and with proper planning, you should be able to minimize your cash outlay for taxes due on the sale of your business. There are three tax areas we will explore:

1. Tax deferred exchange.

2. Installment sale.

3. Allocation of selling price.

There may be other tax savings you can take advantage of. The main point here is, *plan ahead* for maximum tax savings when you sell your business.

Tax Deferred Exchange

A tax deferred exchange allows the business owner to trade or exchange one business for another business, deferring all or part of his or her tax until sale of the second (or final) business. In effect, the businessperson is putting what would otherwise be tax monies toward the down payment on the new business.

The concept of a tax deferred exchange is not complex. However, IRS regulations and latest tax rulings can be very complicated, precise, and subject to elaborate interpretation. Any attempt at qualifying for a tax deferred exchange should be handled through a competent exchange attorney supplemented with proper advice from a CPA.

Installment Sale

Does the seller want or need an installment sale? The Installment Sales Revision Act of 1980 radically revises the reporting of gain on installment sales and deferred payment sales. While some key provisions of the new law are effective only for transactions after October 19, 1980, others are effective retroactively, to transactions already made. Here is a comparison of the law on installment and other deferred payment sales of real property and nondealer sales of personal property, as it existed before the changes were made by the 1980 Act and as it exists after the 1980 Act amendments.

Old Law	New Law
No more than 30% of the selling price can be received in the taxable year of sale.	30% rule eliminated. Amount of payment in year of sale irrelevant. 30% rule dropped retroactively for certain sales.
The contract price must be payable in two or more taxable years.	Only requirement is that at least one payment be made in a taxable year after year of sale. Rule requiring payments in two or more years dropped retroactively for certain sales.
Selling price of personal property must be more than $1,000.	No minimum sale price required.
Installment method must be elected.	Installment treatment automatic unless taxpayer elects not to have installment treatment apply.
Case law upheld installment sale treatment for installment sales to family members who later sold property outright (tax-deferred for first seller; tax-free for second).	Taxes first seller when second seller collects, with some exceptions.
Installment treatment is available for installment sales of depreciable property to family members.	Where taxpayer sells depreciable property to his or her spouse or certain 80% owned corporations or partnerships, deferred payments will be deemed to be received in the taxable year in which the sale occurs, unless absence of tax motive can be shown.
For purposes of reporting gain, like-kind property received in	Like-kind property that can be received without recognition of

Old Law	New Law
an installment sale qualifies for nonrecognition treatment. The value of the like-kind property, however, is included in the contract price and is treated as payment received (e.g., in applying the 30% test), for purposes of reporting profit under the installment rules.	gain is not treated as payment and is not included in the contract price for purposes of reporting profit under the installment method.
On installment sale of corporation's assets in a 12-month, Code Sec. 337 liquidation, distribution of installment obligations to shareholders does not qualify for installment reporting in their hands.	Distribution of installment sale obligations to shareholders in a Code Sec. 337 liquidation will not be taxed to them until the shareholders receive payment on the installment obligation.
Sales with a contingent sales price do not qualify for installment sale treatment.	Installment sale rules apply to sales with a contingent sales price.
It is unclear whether income is realized (as installment obligation disposition) by gift cancellations of the obligation or the installments as they come due.	The cancellation of an installment obligation is treated as a disposition of the obligation by the holder of the obligation.
It is unclear whether any unreported gain remaining at the death of the seller is taxed if the installment obligation is left to the obligor, because the interests of the obligor and obligee merge.	The installment obligation disposition rules can't be avoided by the bequest of an obligation to the obligor. Thus, if an installment obligation is transferred by bequest to the obligor or is cancelled by the executor, the unreported gain becomes taxable to the seller's estate.
A decedent's estate is not allowed to succeed to the tax	An executor or beneficiary who receives a secured installment

Old Law	New Law
treatment which would have been available to the decedent had he or she lived to receive a reconveyance of real property in partial or full satisfaction of purchase money debt. This tax treatment, available when the holder of the obligation is alive, provides for limited recognition of gain.	obligation from a decedent succeeds the decedent for purposes of qualifying for nonrecognition treatment if the real property sold by the decedent is reacquired in cancellation of the obligation.
Standby letter of credit used to secure payment held by court to be payment.	Third party guarantee (including a standby letter of credit) not taken into account in determining if buyer's evidence of indebtedness constitutes payment to seller.
Must carry an interest charge of at least 7% per annum simple interest.	Must carry an interest charge of at least 9% per annum simple interest.

Check your individual state to see if it has conformed to the federal act.

An installment sale normally benefits both buyer and seller. The buyer's down payment is lower than a full cash sale, and the seller pays taxes in a lower tax bracket, while spreading taxable gain over a period of years. There are many factors affecting an installment sale. Buyer, seller, and their accountants and attorneys should all carefully review any installment sale transaction.

Allocation of the Selling Price (tax rules for Business Opportunities)

Under the 1986 tax act, there is no difference in the tax rate for capital gains and ordinary income. You must allocate the purchase price or the Internal Revenue Service will do it for you, and in most cases, years later. Compliance with IRS regulations requires that the business selling price be divided (allocated) between depreciable and non-depreciable categories. Allocations are negotiable (within reason) and could have important tax consequences. The buyer may want maximum allocation to expense categories for maximum tax write off in the year of purchase. The seller wants maximum allocation to capital gain categories for minimum tax consequences on the sale of the business. The selling price of the business would typically be divided among the following categories. (For quick reference table see page 161.)

The following is a very short synopsis. For in depth information, consult a tax accountant.

Accounts receivable
Buyer: Ordinary gain or loss as accounts are paid.
Seller: Straight tax on gains.

Inventory   (finished goods, work in progress, and raw materials)
Buyer: Ordinary gain or loss as inventory is sold.
Seller: Straight tax on gains.

Furniture, fixtures, and equipment
Buyer: A high allocation is advantageous to the buyer because it provides him or her with a higher basis for depreciation. When valuing the furniture, fixtures, and equipment, remember that if the parties agree to a full replacement value, the buyer will have a large tax write-off (full depreciation).
Seller: Straight tax on gains.

Leasehold improvements
Buyer: A high allocation is beneficial to the buyer. The cost of the improvements is amortized over the remaining life of the lease. It is classified as a 1231 asset. Buyer pays no sales tax.
Seller: Straight tax on gains.

Franchises, trademarks, and trade names   (license to use a business name, equipment, or technique). Although they may appear to

be costly, the benefit of using the business name, equipment, or
technique should reflect in higher gross sales than if one operated as a
"lone wolf" business owner.

To establish a value, it is necessary to estimate the amount of additional net profit derived from use of the name, less the cost for use of
the name. This "extra profit" may then be projected over a business's
"life" and discounted back to a present value at an estimated inflation
rate.

A franchise license should have a "going rate" on the open market.
Talk to the franchise or licensing company and franchised business
owners to determine the "going rate" in a particular area.

Tax consequences:
Seller: If seller abandons all right and interest, he or she can write this
off as a tax loss.
Buyer: No effect; buyer cannot claim anything.
Seller: If seller sells all rights and interests to buyer, seller pays
straight tax on gains.

ABC License
Buyer: A low allocation is beneficial to the buyer. The cost of the
license is an investment expense with no amortization.
Seller: Straight tax on gains.

Goodwill   Most people consider Goodwill to be a mysterious category where much of a business's true value lies. It is in this category
that a seller assigns a value to his or her "blood, sweat, and tears"
expended while building the business. It is in this category that a
buyer takes most objection to the "arbitrary" value assigned to the
business by the seller. Goodwill has a value. The logic in arriving at
Goodwill value must be valid and understandable to both buyer and
seller before an agreement can be reached. Goodwill value is related
to net profit and risk. Net profit represents a return in salary for the
time and effort invested by the owner of the business, as well as a
return on the owner's investment in the business. Excess net profit is a
return from the business as a result of: length of time in business,

competitive position, customers, location, business name and reputation, products, service, and various other intangible factors.

Tax consequences:
This is an intangible commodity and difficult to justify. A low allocation is of benefit to the buyer. "Goodwill" is carried on the books as a nondepreciable asset, and as such cannot be written off for tax purposes. The sale of Goodwill results in either gain or loss to the seller.

Covenant not to compete   The seller covenants to the buyer, his or her successors, assignees, and representatives that the seller will not engage, directly or indirectly, in any business the same as, similar to, or in competition with the business within a radius of (number of miles) from the principal place of business being sold for a period of (number of months, years) from date of buyer's possession, either as a principal, agent, manager, employee, owner, partner, stockholder, director or officer of a corporation, trustee, consultant or otherwise in any capacity whatsoever. The covenant is not transferable or assignable.

Tax consequences:
Buyer: Able to amortize cost over term of covenant.
Seller: Straight tax on gains.

Lease valuation   A lease is an exclusive right to use space or equipment at a predetermined rental rate for a specific period of time. When a lease gives a right of use for other than the economic or "going market rate" (above or below), it has a residual value (negative or positive).

The annual lease residual may be calculated by subtracting the annual lease rate from the annual "market rate." This lease residual amount is then multiplied by the remaining lease term to establish the total dollar amount of the lease residual (less lease adjustments). Because of the value of money over time, only a portion of the lease residual amount will be a valid allowance in calculating its present value to the business.

A shortcut appraisal method is to apply a one-year residual dollar amount toward the lease value, using Goodwill calculations to account for additional savings over the remaining lease term. (Where there are large savings for long terms, the "Theory of Value: Lease Residual" technique should be used in determining the value of lease residuals. See page 74.

Tax consequences:
Buyer: A high allocation is of benefit to the buyer. The cost of the lease is amortized over the remaining life of the lease. It is classified as a 1231 asset.
Seller: Straight tax on gains.

Real property   The sale of real property should be handled separately from the sale of the business. Tax benefits and consequences of real property will be separated from business operations on buyer's and seller's tax returns. The buyer may use the allocated amount as his or her tax basis for depreciation. For the seller, there is straight tax on the gains.

Customer list(s)   Present customers mean future income to a business. Therefore, customer lists have a value. The value of a customer list to a business depending on regular repeat sales is much higher than to a business with a low dependency on repeat sales. The value of a customer list is related to the percentage amount of extra annual net income attributable to the list. This dollar amount is then multiplied by the estimated "life" of the list. This list lasts usually from three to five years, but no longer than the period of the covenant not to compete. Because of the time value of money, only a portion of the customer list contribution will be a valid allowance in calculating the list's present value to the business. A quick way to estimate the value of the list is to add on one year's extra net profit (attributable to the list) to account for additional value over the life of the list due to Goodwill calculations. Where there are large extra net profits or unusual conditions in the transaction, the "Theory of Value: Lease Residual" technique should be used in determining the value of customer lists.

Tax consequences:
This list must be separately identified for purposes of allocation similar to the covenant not to compete. Both the buyer and seller must agree on a period of useful life to enable the buyer(s) to amortize its cost as an ordinary expense, provided the IRS agrees the list has a "determinable life." The seller pays straight tax on the gains.

Customer contract(s) Where a contract is guaranteed for a useful life and income, a buyer can amortize the cost of the contract against ordinary income. The seller pays straight tax on the gains.

Quick Tax Effect of the Allocation of the Purchase Price on the Buyer

	For favorable tax effect on buyer*
Accounts receivable	High allocation. Recoverable as collected.
Inventory	High allocation. Recovered as a cost of goods sold.
Furniture, fixtures, and equipment	High allocation. Purchase price recaptured through depreciation.
Leasehold improvements	High allocation. Purchase price can be recouped through amortization over remainder of lease.
Franchises, trademarks, and trade names	Depends on condition of transfer.
ABC License	Low allocation. No deduction allowed.
Goodwill	Low allocation. No deduction allowed.
Covenant not to compete	High allocation. Purchase price can be recouped through amortization.
Lease valuation	High allocation. Purchase price can be recouped through amortization over remainder of life.
Real property (building)	High allocation. Purchase price can be depreciated over remaining life of building.

Real property (land)	Low allocation. Land is not depreciable.
Customer lists	High allocation. Purchase price may be amortizable.
Customer contracts	High allocation. Purchase price may be amortized.
Interest on installment payment purchase	High allocation. Treated as business expense.

*None of these allocations benefit the seller because of straight tax on gains.

15

How Do I Find and Keep a Buyer?

Selling your business yourself is a five-step process.

1. Prepare three presentation packages on your business

a. *Information for Telephone Presentation:* In the early stages of trying to sell your business it is not wise to disclose too much information to casual telephone callers. You will not want customers, building owners, creditors, and suppliers to get upset about a potential change in the operation of the business. Change represents a potential threat to them.

It is best to limit your telephone information. Don't divulge the name and address of your business, but do include the following:

1. Approximate location
2. Type of business
3. Approximate sales
4. Approximate income
5. Approximate amount of cash investment required from the buyer
6. Reason for selling

For a "buyer prequalification questionnaire," ask for the following: (At this point don't forget that if you are giving information it is not unreasonable for you to get some information too.)

1. Name and telephone number
2. Desired location
3. Expectations of salary and net profit
4. Type of business desired
5. Experience
6. Cash available for investment

b. *Information Summary Package:* This is to be mailed to prospective buyers. Include all of paragraph a. above; now start detailing the information but without divulging the name and exact location of your business.

1. Profit and loss statement summary

2. Terms of sale

3. Terms of leases and notes that can be assumed by the buyer

4. Summary list of assets and total value

5. Future prospects of the business and possible areas of improvements

6. Any other pertinent information

c. *Specific Information Package:* This is for qualified and serious buyers.

1. Complete set of financial (profit and loss statements) and operating statements by month for the previous two years

2. Detailed inventory list (included and not included in sale): fixtures, furniture, equipment, leased improvements, personal property, etc.

3. Customer list

4. Supplier list

5. Copy of lease

6. Copies of equipment leases

7. Lists of other assets

8. Copies of all business contractual agreements, notes, etc.

2. Advertise your business for sale

a. Compose an advertisement about your business that will make your telephone ring. A short ad with interesting facts can do wonders. Include all or part of the following:

1. Type of business

2. General location

3. One or two positive features

4. Estimated net income or gross income or return on the investment

5. Attractive financing conditions and terms

b. Place your advertisement in the "Business for Sale" section of your local newspaper or trade magazine. Run your ad long enough to take advantage of advertising rates, but not so long that your ad becomes "stale" (not over 12 days). If your ad does not bring in the calls, something is wrong. Rewrite your ad or place it elsewhere. (Never repeat the same ad.)

3. Select qualified buyers

a. You will do this first through telephone interviews while presenting your business information for consideration. Your ad has brought the telephone inquiries. Use your telephone presentation outline to be sure you convey all the important facts about your business. Do not go overboard. You will not want to disclose too much information to anyone, nor will you want to appear overly anxious to sell your business. This can scare prospects away!

Here is where you begin to qualify your potential buyer. Fill in a "buyer prequalification outline" as you talk with prospects. This will insure that you get all the information you need about your prospect and will provide a useful record on all your telephone contacts.

As you talk with various people you will quickly learn who is really *interested* and who is really *qualified*.

b. Invite interested qualified prospects to see your business. Ask them to bring a financial statement, credit report, and résumé with them. This will quickly eliminate "duds" who are just telling a good story.

Make your appointments after working hours to avoid distractions and interference. This will allow an inspection of your business without your employees and customers getting upset over the pending sale.

When a prospect arrives at your business, trade your specific information package for the prospect's financial statement, credit report, and résumé. Now you can each spend time absorbing some factual data.

Once you have shown the prospect your business and have answered all the questions so far, it's time to sit down together and go over the business appraisal in detail (Chapter 6). See what objections, if any, the prospect has. At this time, you may not agree about several points on your or the prospect's information packages, or on the appraisal, but you will get a sense that it's time to invite the prospect to make an offer to purchase the business. If the prospect hesitates, he or she probably does not have sufficient information, or is uncomfortable about the facts. Assure the prospect you would only like to sketch out an offer.

4. Negotiate a written offer

Now you can use a purchasing (deposit/receipt) agreement to make the offer. Remember, the purchase agreement must have full disclosure of all material facts, including: complete appraisal; fourteen-step sales allocation; seller's and buyer's terms, conditions, obligations, warrants; Seller's and Buyer's Information Disclosure Statements; Landlord/Mortgagee Soft Fixture Waiver; Advanced Cost Agreement; Corporate Resolutions/minutes, if required; estimated closing cost; and, to protect both parties, complete Escrow Instructions, including the escrow holder's or attorney's duties. (See Chapters 16, 17 and 18.)

All forms can be found in the book "Buying and Selling Business Opportunities" also published by Addison-Wesley. Direct updates are available from American Business Consultants, Inc., 1540 Nuthatch Lane, Sunnyvale, CA 94087.

16

Taking an
Offer and Making
It Work

You are striving for agreement between you and the buyer of your business. Agreement means compromise; compromise means both seller and buyer taking a nonemotional, logical approach toward agreement on each element of the business transaction.

TAKE A LOGICAL APPROACH

Is this possible without creating animosity and dissension between the parties? Not always! If the seller and buyer are unable to negotiate the complete transaction, it will fall through. This is not surprising since most of your goals as seller are opposite from those of the buyer. You want a high price. The buyer wants a low price. You want cash. The buyer wants 100 percent financing. You want price allocation for maximum tax write-off for yourself. The buyer also wants tax write-off. What can you do?

Often you will find you are able to reach agreement on the selling price, only to discover that the terms are unsatisfactory. Once again, start asking questions, review this book, especially Chapter 13, check the buyer's qualifications and resources, review Chapters 14 and 15, take each item in a systematic sequence and negotiate one at a time until the buyer starts to revise a few of the terms. At this point, don't get pushy. If the buyer is a reasonable person and sees you backing off (you still have to be firm) in an effort to compromise, he or she will relax a bit and will usually work it out with you. If you find you are still apart on one or two issues, perhaps you both should agree to work with a third party negotiator to establish a fair and equitable compromise. There are many qualified appraisers, business consultants, business brokers, and arbitrators available. Look in the Yellow Pages.

Some people are unable to enter negotiations without becoming emotional over the transaction. Don't feel bad. This is common! You are selling an important part of your life.

ACCEPT YOUR OWN PERSONALITY

If you do try to sell your business yourself, an emotional approach may scare potential buyers away, leaving you frustrated, unhappy, and without a sale. Be smart enough to recognize and accept your own personality traits. Hire a third party to handle the sale of your business and eliminate much of the stress characteristic in selling your own business (see Chapter 19).

17

Avoiding Legal Problems

There is a saying . . . where two or more people gather, there will be two or more opinions on what to do and how to do it!

There is another saying . . . when a dispute goes to court, the only people who come out ahead are the attorneys!

How do *you* stay away from legal problems? In this chapter we will discuss and briefly outline some simple rules to follow in order to avoid unnecessary entanglements.

PUT EVERYTHING IN WRITING

First, put everything in writing. Verbal agreements are not binding. They may be misinterpreted, misconstrued, missed, and often forgotten. It may seem easier and friendlier to verbally agree with the other party. However, when it comes time for actual performance, the parties involved may "forget" what was agreed upon or may mentally modify the terms of the verbal agreement. The consequences of such agreements are disputes leading to tax and legal problems. By putting everything in writing you will eliminate future misunderstandings and possible law suits.

Remember, most buyers are buying a "job," and there are many "material facts" hidden within the business transaction. You *must not* hold back any of these "facts," such as terms, conditions, warranties, representations, obligations, and so on.

If you are a professional real estate agent, attorney, appraiser, accountant, or escrow agent keep the following in mind at all times: If there is the slightest chance of the buyer saying, after the sale has been finalized, "If I had known that . . . I wouldn't have bought the business," chances are you will lose any court case if it proves to be a "material fact."

MAKE FULL DISCLOSURE

Be certain you have made "full disclosure" and have all "material facts" on hand before you offer the business for sale. Not only do you have a legal obligation to see that the agreement is complete, you also have a moral and ethical obligation. For example, the "allocation of the selling price" must be completed or the IRS will challenge it or will do it for the buyer or seller. Of course if they do it you can bet it will be done to the IRS's advantage.

Business permits and special licenses must be in proper order and in the new buyer's name when he or she opens the door for business. The escrow holder will normally say, "not to be concerned with . . . ," but the new buyer cannot operate legally without them. *Everyone* concerned must realize that you are selling a "going business" and that it must be able to operate legally. Everyone must always remember to protect the public against fraud, misrepresentation, and unethical practices.

REVIEW CONTRACTUAL AGREEMENTS

Next, have your attorney, accountant, and/or tax specialist review your contractual agreements. When you enter into an agreement with another party you have the right to know that the agreement is reasonable and legally binding. A good attorney will detect areas of concern or weaknesses in a contract and advise you when adequate protection is not provided in the agreement. Always ask your attorney to read carefully a draft of any agreement *before* you sign it.

In addition, use an escrow checklist (see Chapter 18) to insure that you have covered the basic requirements for a business bulk sale transfer in accordance with the Uniform Commercial Code of your state. Some careful thought and a few pointed questions to cover city, county, state, and federal government rules and regulations will help insure that important items have not been overlooked in the business transfer.

OTHER PROBLEMS

Other areas that must be specified in writing:

1. That the seller is the legal owner of the business and has full authority to execute the agreement, and warrants that he or she has written authority to do so for all sellers.

2. That title to the assets of the business is free and clear from any liens and encumbrances, except as specified in the purchase contract.

3. That the business premises, improvements, real property, equipment, and machinery will pass all inspections necessary to conduct business at the time of physical possession at the close of escrow.

4. That all property that is necessary in the operation of its business shall be delivered at close of escrow in good working condition and repair, ordinary wear and tear excepted.

5. That the seller is not aware of any facts indicating that any customers intend to cease doing business with the seller or to materially alter the amount of the business currently being done with seller.

6. The seller warrants that he or she has not received notice of any claim, litigation, investigation, or federal, state, or local statute, law, ordinance, or regulation; zoning, or other law, ordinance, or regulation affecting the operation of the business or any of the assets being sold, whether real or personal property.

7. That the seller will provide a good and valid bill of sale covering the business, free and clear of any liens and encumbrances whatsoever except those specified in the purchase contract.

8. That the seller will provide or will transfer all the licenses and permits necessary to legally conduct and operate the business.

9. That the seller will supply clearance receipts from State Board of Equalization and Department of Benefit Payments before close of escrow.

10. Buyer's and seller's agreement as to how escrow fees and charges will be paid.

These are a few of the problems that need to be covered in your contract. Can you handle them? Seek the advice of professionals. Use forms available from American Business Consultants, Inc.

USE BINDING ARBITRATION

Finally, use binding "all parties" arbitration clauses in every agreement. Arbitration is the submission of a disputed matter for resolution outside the normal judicial system and is very informal. It is often speedier and less costly than courtroom procedures, and arbitration awards can be enforced legally in court.

With arbitration you can avoid much grief. Family and business pressures, and often remorse, set in very quickly, especially when delays arise. It is possible that when delay occurs, one of the parties may have gotten a better offer and may want out, but is delaying the proceedings so the *other* party will withdraw. That way the delaying party is not held liable.

In your contracts, use a clause that states: "Seller and Buyer hereby agree that if either party delays the sale unreasonably during negotiations, including the delay in delivery of any document beyond the date promised, the period of delay shall be automatically added to the close of escrow date in the purchase and sale agreement.

We suggest you consult the American Arbitration Association. (Look in the Yellow Pages for the nearest location.) At least follow their rules and regulations if both parties can agree on an attorney (often simply selected from the telephone book) to act as arbitrator of the dispute. If an agreement as to an attorney cannot be reached, the parties may each select an attorney to represent themselves, and the two attorneys can then agree as to a third attorney as a tie-breaker.

18

Let's Go to Escrow

Congratulations! You have a qualified buyer for your business and you both have come to an agreement on the price of your business and the terms of the sale. It is now necessary to sort out the final details and complete the actual transfer of your business. You should have a neutral third party "stakeholder" to hold funds, prorate accounts, and insure a clear transfer of the business according to instructions provided by and agreed to by you and the buyer.

THE CONTRACT

The contract, by law, must include "full disclosure." That is, *all* the buyer's and seller's complete terms, conditions, representations, and obligations *must be in writing,* with support data for all "material facts." In business opportunities, there are many "contracts" within a sale of a business. As a guideline, the contract must include but is not limited to the following:

1. Business name and fictitious name (doing business as).

2. Buyer's and seller's names and addresses.

3. Seller's agreement to sell and buyer's agreement to buy.

4. Price and terms:

    a. Total purchase price and down payment.

    b. All encumbrances (notes).

    c. Is encumbrance note secured by the business?

    d. Is additional security required?

5. Inventory (at current wholesale cost). How to be purchased?

6. All assets included in sale, such as business records, trade fixtures, furniture, equipment, tools, supplies, leasehold improvements, telephone numbers, customer list, trade name, transferable permits, special licenses, accounts receivable, ABC license, signs, Goodwill, etc.

7. All liabilities, excluding cash, bank accounts, accounts payable, and deposits.

8. Is this an installment sale? Check federal and state laws.

9. Allocation of the selling price.

   a. Accounts receivable

   b. Inventory (at current wholesale cost)

   c. Furniture, fixtures, and equipment (market value installed)

   d. Leasehold improvements (minus used-up life)

   e. Franchises, trademarks, and trade names

   f. ABC license

   g. Goodwill

   h. Covenant not to compete

   i. Lease valuation (residual plus improvements)

   j. Real property (should be a separate purchase agreement)

   k. Customer lists

   l. Customer contracts

   m. Other

10. Seller warrants, represents, and shall provide the following:

   a. Proof that he or she is the legal owner.

   b. Proof that the property is free and clear, except as noted.

   c. Proof that the business will pass all regulatory inspections.

   d. Assurance that business equipment will be in good working condition at time of transfer.

   e. Assurance that there are no claims, litigation, or investigations against the business, other than those which have been disclosed.

   f. Assurance that the business is or is not affected by the special studies zone act.

   g. Assurance that the business is or is not affected by the National Flood Control Act.

h. A good and valid bill of sale.

i. A transfer of all licenses and permits.

j. Clearance receipts from state agencies.

k. Pink slips to any motor vehicles.

l. Assurance to operate business in the same manner until transferred.

m. Assurance that all statements made are true and correct.

n. Training for the buyer (number of hours per day and number of days, and compensation, if any).

o. Authorization for buyer or buyer's broker to contact anyone connected with the business to request information regarding the business.

11. Buyer agrees:

a. To assume lease, option, or new lease.

b. To acknowledge examination and approval of the seller's books, records, and financial statements.

c. To assume all contracts, medical plans, 2-for-1 dinner plans, union contracts, employee contracts, menus, copyrights, patents, trademarks, profit-sharing contracts, royalties, customers lists, formulas, receipts, advertisements, etc.

d. To the transfer of franchise contract. Franchise transfer fees.

e. To the transfer of vending machine games, equipment leases, etc.

f. To approval of lists of furniture, fixtures, and equipment included in sale, not included in sale, and items owned or leased by others.

g. To maintain insurance on equipment to cover any obligation to the seller.

h. To pay sales tax on fixtures and equipment.

i. To buyer's authority to sign agreement.

12. Both parties agree:

   a. To pay half each of escrow and transfer fees.

   b. On lists of furniture, fixtures, and equipment to be sold, not to be sold, and leased by others in writing before the close of escrow.

   c. To make application for transfer of alcoholic beverages control license.

   d. That closing of escrow and day of possession is the same day.

   e. To prorate all personal property taxes, rents, interest charges, insurance, and similar costs, etc.

13. Escrow holder's duties:

   a. Complete transaction in accordance with Bulk Transfer division of the Uniform Commercial Code in your state.

   b. To record and publish transaction in a judicial district newspaper at least twelve business days prior to the date of transfer.

   c. Distribute all monies and documents to the respective parties.

14. Arbitration clause in accordance with American Arbitration Association.

15. Default clauses if seller or buyer fails or refuses to complete agreement.

16. All signatures, titles, and dates.

When all terms and conditions of transfer have been completed, the escrow holder will "close" the escrow on the agreed date and the sale of the business will be complete. The escrow holder disburses all funds from the escrow to creditors of the business and sends you, the seller, a check for the balance as your proceeds from the sale. The escrow holder also sends the bill of sale, all notes, and related documentation to the buyer.

19

The Role of
the Business
Broker

The following details the role of the professional business broker; that is, what the Business Opportunities salesperson must and must not do.

DO'S AND DON'TS

The Business Opportunities salesperson's "must's" This person must:

1. Keep informed of changes in laws, codes, and rules and regulations affecting and related to Business Opportunities, consumer protection, consumer services, real estate, business, professional, civil, administration, revenue and taxation, building and government codes, city and county ordinances, health department, alcoholic beverage control, and many others.

2. Make full disclosures of all "material facts," warranties, representations, obligations, terms, and conditions in writing *before* offering a Business Opportunity for sale.

3. Protect the public against fraud, misrepresentation, and unethical practices.

4. Recommend the use of professionals in all transactions, such as attorneys, accountants, and tax specialists.

5. Recommend arbitration when necessary.

6. Develop business appraisal expertise.

7. Recommend that commissions or fees, where mentioned in agreements, state in a minimum of 10 pt. boldface type: "**Real estate commissions are negotiable and not fixed by law.**"

8. Must disclose to all parties, in advance, when the salesperson is acting for both buyer and seller.

The Business Opportunities salesperson's "must not's" This person must not:

1. Give any legal or tax advice, unless qualified and licensed to do so.

2. Make statements that cannot be verified.

3. Discriminate or deny services or information to any person for reason of race, creed, sex, or national origin.

4. Allow unauthorized sharing of trade secrets or personal or confidential information to other salespeople, clients, competitors, and others, including but not limited to the following information:

   a. Condition of books

   b. Financial statements

   c. Formulas and recipes

   d. Methods of operation

   e. Offers of other parties

   f. Negotiating or soliciting a "listing," knowing it has *not* expired

5. Make false representation, such as:

   a. Advertising phoney or sold business listings

   b. Advertising misleading financial terms

   c. Representing oneself or another agent as a buyer in an attempt to acquire a listing

FIRM AND FAIR POLICY

There are many more parties involved in a Business Opportunity transaction compared to the typical residential sale. Therefore, it is imperative that all parties be handled with the same fair and ethical treatment.

In the typical transaction, an owner who is selling a business is giving up an important part of his or her life. The owner has probably spent many hours, days, and years and a lot of money; and has probably put an enormous amount of creative energy into the business. The buyer, in most cases, is stepping into a world of the unknown. The buyer is asked to exchange his or her worldly fortunes for an item of questionable value.

In short, both buyer and seller are at opposite ends of a spectrum and are under great stress. The Business Opportunities salesperson, therefore, must be very skillful in the role of mediator, and must successfully satisfy the needs and desires of both parties. A "professional counselor" approach or technique is necessary to firmly guide both parties, step by step, through their Bulk Sale Transfer. This normally can be accomplished only if the salesperson successfully educates both parties as they pass through various stages, using ethical business standards of practice and adopting the new Code of Ethics and Professional Conduct by the Department of Real Estate of your state.

The business broker's needs The professional business broker should have access to:

1. Qualified buyers and sellers

2. Certified Business Opportunity appraisers

3. All approved contract forms with all material facts stated within

4. Qualified attorneys, CPA's, accountants, and tax specialists

5. Advertising outlets

6. Multiple listing services

7. Local- and state-wide Business Opportunity exchanges

8. Referral service to other Business Opportunity specialists

The professional broker should conduct an in-depth study of a business operation and its financial status. The broker should study all the costs involved and make recommendations where specific areas need improving: for example, labor, materials, facilities, equipment, and marketing. Last, but not least, the broker should be able to project a return on an investment on past performance.

It is the role of the Business Opportunities salesperson to combine expertise in evaluating businesses, marketing, and financing to put together an attractive sales package on the business for presentation to prospective buyers.

Upon locating qualified buyers, the business broker presents the business in its most attractive light with all material facts presented, obtains offers, and negotiates a contract satisfactory to all parties in the transaction.

It is the Business Opportunities salesperson's responsibility to bring the transaction through the escrow phase to a successful completion.

20

Retired:
What Should
I Do Now?

Now you have completed the business cycle.You have learned how to locate, appraise, finance, and operate a business to your liking. Look how you made it grow and prosper! Then you sold your business for a nice profit; now you can afford to sit back and take it easy for awhile. Retired? What should you do now?

Fortunately, there are many opportunities for the successful businessperson who has assets. Many people desire a chance to relieve such a successful person of his or her loose cash.

Your decision to retire becomes a two-edged sword! Don't let yourself or your money sit around doing nothing! You will dry up and blow away along with the money. Friends, relatives, neighbors, even strangers and other fair-weather friends are likely to hassle you by telling you what they can do with *your* money if only you will place it in their care. Nonsense!

INVEST YOUR MONEY

This book shows *you* how to control *your* money. The answer, then, to your retirement is in your own ability to maintain control of your money.

The best way to do this is by investing it. Why not start the cycle over again by locating a business you can build for future profit? Look at it as your retirement hobby. At this point in your life, having owned, operated, managed, and sold one, two, or more businesses, your retirement venture may be the smoothest and easiest operation yet. You know all the ins and outs of Business Opportunities, so why not put your lifelong experience and ability and profits to work for you again?

Because you have owned, managed, and successfully sold your business, you are of course in a better position to look closely at one or more businesses. This time, however, instead of operating the business yourself you can afford to hire a manager to supervise the overall operation. All you need to do is spend a few hours a week making sure your new investment is functioning smoothly. The rest of the time you can spend on those extended vacations you have dreamed of and worked for all your life.

INCREASE YOUR KNOWLEDGE

At this point you may feel the need for additional help in appraising, buying, operating, and selling your own business. Please refer to the list in Appendix II, select several items, and check with American Business Consultants, Inc., (Sunnyvale, California) as to where and when their seminars will be held (in most major cities). By all means attend the popular seminars, "How to Buy and Sell Business Opportunities" and "Business Opportunity Appraiser." At these seminars you will learn the secrets of becoming a professional Business Opportunities specialist.

Tax deduction   Tax deductions are allowed for all expenses of continuing education (including registration fees, travel, meals, and lodging) undertaken to maintain and improve professional skills, according to Section 162 of the 1954 Internal Revenue Code, Treas. Reg. 1-162-5 *Coughlin* v. *Commissioner*, 203F 2d 307. If you are unsure about whether or not these seminars and books qualify for you, we advise you to consult your accountant or attorney.

Certificates   All registrants meeting the requirements of each seminar will receive an official state-approved certificate of completion at the conclusion of each course. Currently approved by Department of Real Estate in California, Nevada, South Dakota, Ohio, Kansas, Wisconsin, Connecticut, Maryland, Washington, D.C., Florida, Iowa, and Montana, and Board of Equalization in California.

INVEST YOUR KNOWLEDGE AND EXPERIENCES

With all your direct experiences, this may be your "retirement"—*be a consultant!* You can set your own hours and work habits. There are many opportunities open in this field:

Business appraiser Appraise businesses for probate, dissolution of businesses, dissolution of marriages, contested business valuations, partner-stockholder buy-outs, mergers and/or acquisitions, lease value, testifying in court as a qualified "expert witness."

Business consultant Government regulations, time management, business profiles, identifying business frauds, identifying business opportunities, releases, resumés, business insurance, security agreements, covenant-not-to-compete agreements, lease agreements, and increase present business.

Business broker Purchase or sale of a business, location of a business, special license and permit transfer, key contacts, making an offer, handling counter-offers, handling purveyors, advertising, negotiating for all parties, trust deeds, property owners, handling bulk sale transactions, acting as escrow agent, Uniform Commercial Code requirements, and ABC liquor regulations.

Financial consultant Working with banks, Small Business Administration, private financiers, raising capital, encumbrances (notes), installment notes, creative financing, accounts payable, accounts receivable, payroll, tax consequences, inventory control, allocation of selling price, equipment purchases and/or leases, analyzing financial records, books, profit and loss statements, and cash flow vs. true net profits.

As you can see, it's wide open—not for everyone—but surely within the above possibilities.

The satisfaction of helping others is rewarding in itself. You can achieve a degree of personal happiness and accomplishment while becoming a true professional and a credit to your family and community. Please write to us and keep us informed of your progress. We will keep you up to date with new books, concepts, business trends, and rules, regulations, and laws affecting your business.

Good hunting! And good luck in your business venture!

21

How to Get
100 Percent
Free Advertising

The following are tried and proved simple ways to get free advertising for your services and products. Almost any product or service may be advertised in this way. (Check local ordinances and laws; they may prohibit, or require licenses.)

Free Advertising

There are several advertisers that offer free advertising and you pay per response or percentage of profit basis. (Some have a nominal cost to produce the ad or commercial.)

1. *Publications:*
   a. Parade Publications, Inc., 750 Third Ave., N.Y., N.Y. 10017; 30¢ per response; if required to send money, it is 75¢ per response.
   b. Many companies have a free publication for their employees.
   c. T.V. Facts, a weekly television magazine. Free community bulletin board service.

2. *T.V.:*
   a. OGI Marketing, 114 E. 32nd St., N.Y., N.Y. 10016; percentage of profit, including an 800 number (toll-free).
   b. Ralph Lopatin Productions, Inc., 1728 Cherry Hill St., Phila., PA 19103; guaranteed nominal production cost ($4,900).
   c. Nationwide T.V. Marketing, Inc., 2700 River Rd., Des Plaines, IL 60018; percentage of profit basis.
   d. Tele-Star Marketing, 99 W. Hawthorne Ave., Valley Stream, N.Y. 11580; percentage of profit basis.

3. *T.V., Radio, and Magazines:*

   Monitor Marketing Corp., 880 Third Ave., N.Y., N.Y. 10022; sales commission.

4. *Syndicated News Services:*

   Astroline, Box 177, Midway City, CA 92655.

5. *Special Discount Rates—National Publications:*

   Winthrop Mail Service, P.O. Box 5882, Sarasota, FLA 33579; per display inch = $37.50–500,000 readership.

6. *Bonus Method:*

Write to Progressive Publications, Box 3770, Clearlake Highlands, CA 95422 for a free copy of their "Progressive Classified Bulletin." They offer free advertising if your products or services appeal to the mail order trade. Circulation averages about 5,000 per month, and you must agree to mail fifty copies each issue in exchange for the free ads. These are strictly classified ads so no camera-ready copy is required. They also offer a *free* review of your offer in their "Progressive Newsletter," which is mailed only to active mail dealers each issue. To qualify for this free review you must provide them with sample copies of your product and complete details of your offer.

Human Interest Story

Write about yourself and your business and submit it to the city desk of your local newspaper and to leading magazines. If it is exceptional, they may even pay you. Many newspapers will have "community board" columns to carry your story.

News Release

Make an announcement about your company or services:

1. Appointing officers, or new officers
2. Promotions
3. New address, etc.

Literature

Place circulars, sales letters, and announcements on bulletin boards found in dozens of places around town—markets, barber shops, schools, etc. A good method is to set up a "take-one" box and stuff it with 3 x 6 circulars.

Place literature on car windshields in parking lots. A product or service that appeals to the general public will provide the greatest response, especially on weekends. One salesman who was offering recreational land had flyers printed and distributed by his own kids every weekend during the prime selling months. He reported sales from these flyers totaling almost $500,000 his first year.

Leave literature on doorsteps of residences and businesses in your area. The same land salesman added this method his second year and increased sales by an additional $200,000. If you are lazy hire kids to make the deliveries and pay them 1¢ per flyer; it's cheap coverage. Go to a church or civic group, ask them to deliver your literature in exchange for a donation of money as a "contribution" to their organization. (Tax deduction? Check with your accountant.)

Free Postage

1. In all cases be sure to place this note within your ad—"SASE"— which means send a "self-addressed stamped envelope," this way you save the postage and envelope cost.

2. Mail for others at a price. Run an ad: "Your circulars mailed to good prospects. 100 8½ x 11 . . . 75¢. Send circulars and stamped envelopes to (your name and address)." Stuff your circulars and your customers' circulars into the 100 envelopes and address them to good mutual prospects. Not only will you get orders from your circulars but your customers will get orders from their circulars.

3. Look for the code letters X100SYMF on mail order circulars or ads. It means "exchange 100 circulars. Send yours, mine will follow." Do the same on all outgoing mail. Soon you will be getting a number of exchange circulars to mail. Exchange your circulars with other dealers. Offer to mail their circulars if they will mail your circulars. If you can get several dealers that you can rely on then you can get your circulars mailed for free on a regular basis.

4. If you mail 200 or more of the same size and weight, you can use U.S. Postal "bulk rate" which is only 12.5 each or "nonprofit bulk rate" at 8.5 each versus 22¢ each—quite a savings in a year. Check with your post office.

Free Printing and Make Money Too

1. Find a printer who charges $12.00 to print 1,000 9 × 12's on both sides. Now plan an ad; "1,000 3 × 6 circulars printed for only $3.00. Send $3.00 and stamped envelopes to (your name and address)." You will get 6 circulars on each side, 6,000 for yourself and 1,000 each for your 6 customers, and you have made $6.00 on the deal. ($18.00 collected and only $12.00 to print).

2. Combine number 1 above with number 2 under "Free Postage." You get free printing and free postage for your circulars.

How to get 25¢ each for mailing out 1,000 envelopes or $1,000 for 4,000 envelopes or how to mail out 1,000 big mails a month at no cost

This is a plan that can pull in the quarters for you. Simply run an ad like the following: "How to get 25¢ each for mailing out 1,000 envelopes a month. My big mail included all for 25¢." This should start the mail rolling. This plan will save you money from buying a name list say for $15.00 a 1,000. You would also have to buy 1,000 stamps, another $220.00 savings, plus all the printing offers you included in your package. You can really see just what this one little maneuver can do when you have a good pulling ad. You can bet these names will be of far better quality than a bought list.

You can use or sell these plans to bring in the quarters; then always fill your envelopes to the brim or take advantage of the postage situation and put as many advertising circulars in the envelope as the postage will allow. You probably wouldn't make much money this way, but you are accumulating a very valuable buying list of names, with which you can start a selling names list. This would be as good a name list as would possibly be available to you by any other means; this would provide you with an inquisitive looking group of people where the list is definitely not overworked.

You see, this is how you can make up a big mail list free—by including your big mail as a free rider by filling your envelope, along with your regular plans. Work this plan for extra profits.

How to Write Advertisements That Produce Results! The "Why" Method

Here is the method for writing the perfect advertisement. As you are writing your ad, keep asking the question WHY. Why should people buy my product? Why does my product save money? Why does my product make money? Why is my price what it is? Why is my product a quality product? Why should people buy it from me? If you can answer all your *why* questions in your advertisement, then you have an ad which will most likely be a powerful profit puller.

22

Tax Planning and Tax Savings

December 31 closes off your opportunities to do anything about your tax picture, but by intelligent planning and the right action during October through December you may be able to realize substantial tax savings.

The following is based on the year beginning January 1, 1986, but it will give you some suggestions and pointers with the aim to save you tax dollars and to help you avoid some pitfalls. Our main objective is to increase your tax awareness and as a result prompt you to take steps to decrease your taxes in any year. Obviously there is much more to tax planning than what is covered here. We urge you to seek competent counsel and an accountant if you have a situation such as sale of real estate, business, or stock, retirement (or are contemplating it), marriage, divorce, substantially increased or decreased income, or a multitude of other events that could give rise to a changed tax picture.

Year-end tax planning normally requires that a calculation be made of your projected taxable income for a calendar year using reasonable estimates, which could be based in part on your information on your last two tax returns. The anticipated financial transactions from October and during the next twelve months should then be categorized in order to isolate those that can be controlled (i.e., those transactions that can be completed this tax year, before December 31, or put off until next year January 2).

Once the above information has been assembled you can then determine the projected tax liability that will occur in each year and determine what steps can be taken to *minimize the combined tax liability of both years.*

The principles used in minimizing your tax liability include:

a. *Shifting income or deductions or both* from one year to another in order to minimize the *overall* tax burden.

b. *Deferring* the payment of tax.

c. Taking advantage of all *allowable deductions.*

1. PLANNING FOR INCOME

a. *Income Deferral*

The deferral of income from this tax year to the next taxable year may accomplish both of the following objectives:

1. Defer the payment of income tax.

2. Reduce the overall tax liability for the two years as a result of determinable lower tax brackets anticipated for next year.

The deferral of income may be accomplished any number of ways, including the following:

1. If you report income on the cash basis, accelerate the payment of business or deductible expenses.

   (Check if you can use the cash method. It is available to all businesses with sales under $5,000,000; but not to sub-S corporations.)

2. Cash basis taxpayers may also delay mailing bills or invoices thus delaying the collection of income.

3. If you are contemplating the sale of an asset before the end of the year, and payment of the sales price is to be received over a period of years, you can elect to pay tax on the gain as you receive payments, rather than all in the year of sale.

2. PLANNING FOR ITEMIZED DEDUCTIONS

a. *Zero Bracket Amount (Standard Deduction)*

All taxpayers (except for dependents claimed on another return) are entitled to a "fixed standard deduction." For single taxpayers the deduction is $2,540 in 1987 and $3,000 in 1988. Heads of household may deduct $2,540 in 1987 and $4,000 in 1988. Married couples may deduct $3,760 in 1987 and $5,000 in 1988. For married taxpayers filing separately, the deduction is $1,880 in 1987 and $2,500 in 1988.

Therefore, if your itemized deductions for the year will approximate or fall below the zero bracket amount allowed, you should review your itemized deductions paid to date and determine whether you should accelerate or defer payment of itemized deductions during the rest of the year. By claiming the zero bracket amount in one year and itemizing deductions in another year, you may be able to create a substantial increase in total deductions claimed for the two years. The value of personal exemptions is $1,900 in 1987, $1,950 in 1988, and $2,000 in 1989.

b. *Itemized Deductions Which May Be Accelerated or Deferred (Controllable)*

If you wish to utilize itemized deductions in the year of greatest income, or to defer for one year paying taxes, you should carefully consider the specific recommendations that follow:

1. *Prepayment of state income tax deduction:* If you forecast a significant balance due with your present state income tax return, you may wish to increase your estimated tax payment and instead of paying the fourth quarter state estimated tax payment in January, you should consider making payment prior to December 31.

2. *Property taxes:* You may wish to pay ahead of due date (April 10) your 2nd installment of your real estate taxes. By paying these taxes before December 31, you will substantially increase your tax deduction.

3. *Charitable contributions:* November and December are traditional months for giving. This applies to gifts to churches or other charities. Now may be a good time to accelerate your pledge or commitment to your church and get increased tax savings. Don't forget that donations of used clothing, furniture, or other items to Goodwill and other charities are deductible to the extent of the fair market value of the property. The organizations should provide you with a receipt of your contributions. Also, out-of-

pocket expenses and automobile mileage (at 12¢ per mile) on behalf of charities are deductible, subject to a percent limitation.

4. *Medical expenses:* If your medical expenses paid to date exceed 7.5 percent of your projected adjusted gross income, make sure all outstanding doctor, dentist, hospital, and drug bills are paid by December 31, because next year these expenses might not exceed the income limitation and would therefore not be deductible.

Taxpayers who own stock in a closely-held corporation, and are employed by the corporation, should consider having the corporation establish a nondiscriminatory *"Medical Reimbursement Plan."* The corporation in most cases could pay all medical, dental, and drug expenses of a covered employee (you) and your dependents and deduct the entire amount, without regard to the 1 percent or 3 percent income limitations, and the covered employee does not have to report the payments as income.

5. *Multiple support agreement (form 2120):* It can apply when no single person supplies more than half of the dependent's support, but together, two or more persons provide over the required 50 percent. They must agree among themselves that only one will claim the exemption.

3. CAPITAL GAINS AND LOSSES

a. *Timing*

If you wish to recognize a loss this year from the sale of a security, the sale may be executed through December 31. But gain transactions must be executed by December 21, unless the sale is a cash sale.

b. *Designating the Securities Sold*

If you purchase several blocks of a security and are only selling a portion of your holdings, make sure you deliver the block

that gives you the most advantageous tax treatment. If you are
selling at a gain, you would usually want to sell the block which
has been held for more than twelve months and has the highest cost.

c. *Child Care Credit*

A direct tax credit may be claimed by a taxpayer equal to 20
percent of the qualified expenses paid for the care of certain
qualifying dependents (including a spouse incapable of self-
care). The maximum tax savings is $480 to $720 for one child,
$960 to $1,440 for two or more children. Where one spouse is
either employed part-time or is a student, the allowable credit
may be reduced. This credit is available no matter how high a
person's income may be.

4. DEDUCTIONS AVAILABLE WHETHER OR NOT YOU ITEMIZE

a. *Individual Retirement Account (IRA)*

An individual who is not covered by a pension or profit sharing plan can contribute up to 15 percent of his or her salary
or earned income to a special savings account, mutual fund,
or investment account, to produce a maximum deduction of
$2,000. If his or her spouse does not work, the maximum may
be increased to $2,250 under an IRA plan whereby half of the
contribution is specifically earmarked for the spouse's benefit.
This is subject to certain gross income limitations.

Several points of caution should be noted:

1. The payment must be made no later than the due date of
   your return. If you don't have a plan you can set it up on
   or before April 15 (or later if you have a valid extension);

2. If money is withdrawn from the IRA or is used to secure a
   loan prior to your reaching age fifty-nine and one-half, regular income tax will be incurred, plus a 10 percent penalty
   tax; and

3. Shop carefully before selecting your IRA custodian. Determine in advance the interest rate you will earn (if a savings plan is used) and the fees charged "up front," annually, and/or a time of distribution.

b. *Keogh Plans for Self-Employed Individuals and Partnerships*

Self-employed individuals and business partnerships should consider establishing or contributing to a "Keogh Plan" (a retirement plan for self-employed individuals and their eligible employees). Twenty-five percent (25%) of net income can be contributed, up to a maximum of $30,000 (if a defined benefit Keogh Plan is adopted) for each person, and the entire amount is deductible.

A contribution to a Keogh Plan which is in existence as of December 31, may be funded any time before the due date of the tax return and still be claimed on the contributor's this year individual income tax return. If there is any doubt as to the maximum allowable contribution, we recommend a partial contribution now and the balance early next year.

5. FEDERAL AND STATE WITHHOLDING OR ESTIMATED TAX

In general, substantial penalties will be assessed if your withholding and/or estimated tax payments will be less than 90 percent of this year's tax. However, these underpayment penalties can be eliminated if any one of our exceptions apply. The most common exception is when your current year's withholding and/or quarterly estimated tax payments equal your total last year income liability. You should cover any deficiency prior to January 15 next year. However, you could still be penalized for paying an insufficient amount on the first three estimated installments.

6. TAX EFFECTS OF MARRIAGE OR DIVORCE

In general, a person's marital status as of the end of the year determines whether or not a joint tax return can be filed. A decision as to whether or not to marry or dissolve a marriage this year will have a direct impact on the combined tax liabilities of the partners. Where only one party has significant *income, being married and filing a joint tax return will generally be more beneficial than filing separate returns.* Alternatively, where both parties have significant income the use of the "single" rates may produce a more favorable combined tax liability.

7. SALE OF PERSONAL RESIDENCE BY TAXPAYERS OVER AGE 55

Taxpayers fifty-five or over who sell their home at a gain and do not buy another home, get a big tax break. If a taxpayer over fifty-five used his or her home as the principal residence three out of the five years immediately preceding the sale, he or she may exclude up to $125,000 of the profit once in his or her lifetime. If you are fifty-three or fifty-four years old and contemplating the sale of your home in the near future and don't plan to reinvest the proceeds in a replacement house, you may want to defer the sale until you reach age fifty-five to take advantage of this provision of the new law.

8. TRAVEL AND ENTERTAINMENT EXPENSES, INDIVIDUAL AND CORPORATE RETURNS

a. *General Requirements*

The deduction of travel or entertainment expenses requires additional documentation in order to support the claimed deduction. For example, in order to claim an entertainment expense, contemporaneous records should be maintained documenting the following: (1) who was entertained, (2) the amounts and nature of the expenditure, (3) where the entertainment was incurred, (4) when the entertainment was incurred, (5) and the business discussed or the purpose of the entertainment. Maintenance of a daily "diary" is the best evidence to present an IRS agent in support of these deductions.

In addition, when an individual expenditure exceeds $25, a receipt would be required. There is an 80% limitation on travel, entertainment, and meals away from your offfice.

b. *Tax Return Preparer Requirements*

The Tax Reform Act of 1986 requires, under penalty, that a tax preparer disclose directly on a return when unsupported estimated amounts are deducted as travel and entertainment. This includes "per diem" estimates, as well as other unreimbursed and unsupported amounts. As this disclosure could possibly "flag" your return for audit, we strongly urge that you maintain records of both travel and entertainment expenditures in order to claim a deduction on your business or personal return.

9. MISCELLANEOUS

a. *Optional Mileage Rate*

The optional mileage rate for business use has increased from 18.5 cents to 21 cents for the first 15,000 miles. It is 11 cents for the miles driven beyond 15,000 miles.

b. *Year-end Gifts*

If you have made no gifts so far this year and are a potential donor, you have the opportunity to take advantage of the annual gift tax exclusion allowable for the first $10,000 in gifts to each donee. Once the year is over, there is one less annual exclusion per donee available to you.

c. *Moving Expenses*

You may deduct the reasonable expenses of moving to another location if the move is incidental to your beginning full-time employment in a new location. The distance between your new place of employment and your former residence must be at least 35 miles farther than the distance from your former residence to your prior place of work. The mileage rate is only 9 cents per mile.

Income averaging and investment tax credit have been repealed.

If you have a refund due, file in January. Inflation is eating up the value of every dollar of it, and Uncle Sam isn't paying any interest. The earlier you file, the sooner you can put that money to work.

Here are several questions that need "hard" answers. See your tax accountant, CPA, Financial Management Service, attorney and/or insurance specialist.

a. *Personal Planning*
   What are your priorities?

   1. Capital accumulation

   2. Estate tax and liquidation planning

   3. Family income protection

   4. Disability income

   5. Spouse insurance

   6. Mortgage insurance

   7. Children's life insurance

   8. Term insurance conversion

   9. Will and trust planning

   10. Retirement planning

   11. Charitable and family gifts

   12. Educational needs

   13. Tax shelters

b. *Business Planning*

   1. What is my business worth today versus its value if I died or were disabled?

2. What would my family do with my business if I died today?

3. What are the tax consequences to me and my business if my wife/husband should die today?

4. Do I have current buy/sell agreement with my partners or stockholders that will ensure both business continuity and adequately protect my family's interest in the business if I should die today?

5. Am I maximizing the personal tax advantages available to me through my business?

6. Do I have a Medical Reimbursement or Salary Continuation Plan? A Section 79 deductible insurance plan?

7. Would a Section 303 Stock Redemption Plan fit my business and personal needs?

8. Am I taking advantage of a qualified retirement plan such as IRA, Keogh, or pension and profit sharing? If so, do I have the proper type of plan for myself and my business?

9. Should I incorporate my business, and if so, would a conventional corporation or hybrid best fit my situation?

10. Does my corporation have an excess accumulated earnings problem, and if so, what can I do to solve it?

Appendix I
Definitions

Title in Business Opportunities

Severalty   Single.

Co-ownership   Two or more persons.

Tenancy in common   Two or more persons holding an undivided interest in the same property.

Joint tenancy   Same as tenancy in common, but if one party dies, his or her title passes to the surviving part or parties by operation of law; each must have an equal share.

Community property   Shared ownership acquired by husband and wife.

Forms of Business Entity in
Business Opportunities

Sole proprietorship   The sole owner of a business (one individual). The owner is personally liable for the debts of the business.

Partnership   A business owned by two or more persons. Each partner is personally liable for the debts of the partnership.

Limited partnership   Consists of one or more general partners who run the business and incur personal liability for partnership debts, and one or more limited partners who incur no personal liability for partnership debts. However, a limited partner cannot take part in managing the partnership.

Joint venture   Two or more persons. Same as partnership except that it exists to undertake a single project.

Corporation   A legal entity separate from the persons who own, control, manage, and operate it. Liability of the owner(s) or shareholder(s) is limited to the assets of the corporation.

More Common Definitions in Business Opportunities

Agent   One acting under authority of a principal to do the principal's business. The agent must use his or her best efforts and keep the principal fully informed of all material facts.

Arbitration   The submission of a disputed matter for resolution outside the normal judicial system. It is often speedier and less costly than courtroom procedures. An arbitration award can be enforced legally in court: if one or more parties cannot agree on a single arbitrator, they can select arbitrators under the rules of the American Arbitration Association.

Bulk-sale law   Provisions of the Uniform Commercial Code that regulate the sale of inventory of a business for the protection of the seller's creditors.

Capital gain   The gain received on the sale of real or personal property (Goodwill, stocks, bonds, etc.), other than property sold as stock-in-trade.

Capitalization   Determination of the value of property by considering its net income and return on investment.

Cash flow   Income remaining after deducting from gross income, all operating expenses, including loan payments and an allowance for the income tax attributable to net income.

Contract   An agreement freely reached to do or not to do a certain thing, for the breach of which the law provides a remedy. It may be written or oral, but whenever possible should be written, especially where real property is involved. To be enforceable, the contract should contain all essential terms and conditions and should convey the same meaning to each party.

Defamation   Injury to a person's business or personal character or reputation resulting from libelous or slanderous conduct.

Depreciation/Appreciation   Depreciation is a loss in value due to any cause. Appreciation is the opposite, a gain in value due to any cause.

Fiduciary relationship A relationship of trust and responsibility existing between two people as from financial matters. The principal may legally trust and depend upon his or her agent to be honest and faithful. The principal may call upon the agent at any time to render an accounting of any funds handled by the agent.

Fraud, deceit, and misrepresentation Intentional or negligent misrepresentation or concealment of a material fact, with justifiable reliance thereon by another party, who is thereby damaged.

Names Ordinarily, unless done to escape punishment or to defraud others, a person has the right to adopt any name he or she chooses. The adopted name is said to become the real name by reputation. Names can also be changed by court proceedings. When the business name is not the name of the individual or individuals who own it, it is usually necessary to register the name so that the public will have a means of associating the trade name with the individual. This is the reason for filing a fictitious name statement (dba—Doing Business As).

Notice of intention to engage in sale of alcoholic beverages Document that must be posted on premises 30 days prior to issuance or transfer of license and must be published once in newspaper of general circulation if on-sale license is required.

Notice of intention to sell (notice to creditors of bulk transfer) Document that should be recorded and published prior to the sale of a Business Opportunity in order to give notice of the impending sale to the seller's creditors.

Notice of intention to transfer business premises Document that must be recorded in county where business premise is located, and filed with the Department of ABC prior to transfer of a liquor license.

Notice to pay rent or quit A three-day notice required by law before a tenant, delinquent in rental payments or other obligations, may be evicted by suit.

Options An agreement to hold an offer open for a specified period of time, usually in consideration for the payment of a certain sum of money. The person granting the option is the optioner. The person receiving the option is the optionee. The optioner cannot withdraw the option before its expiration date. The consideration for an option is not normally returnable to the optionee if he or she fails to exercise the option. If the optionee does exercise the option, the consideration is often applied to the purchase price.

Real-estate exchange   When certain kinds of "like" property are exchanged, Section 1031 of the Internal Revenue Code provides that part or all of the taxes may be deferred. Real estate held for business or as an investment is considered "like" property. For instance, lake-front lots may be exchanged for apartments, retail stores for office buildings, etc., or a combination of income-producing real estate may be exchanged.

Uniform commercial code   The law that establishes a uniform and comprehensive scheme for the regulation of secured transactions in personal property and bulk-sale transfer. This law is designed to protect buyer, seller, and creditors alike in personal property trans-actions. Division 6 covers bulk transfers. Division 9 covers secured transactions.

Zoning   Division of a county, city, or other entity into zones or districts according to permitted use, heights, setback lines, develop-ment, and other factors.

Zoning

	Legal status	Decision maker	Public hearing	Grounds for approval	Chances for approval
A. Rezoning	Area given new zoning classification: Zoning map redrawn.	Town or county usually empowers planning or zoning board to make recommendations or decision. Board's decision can be appealed to council.	Yes. May require 2 or 3 hearings for board recommendation and one for town or council approval.	Zoning will be advantageous to community. (Existing zoning is inappropriate.)	Most difficult form of zoning relief to achieve.
B. Variance	Particular project exempted from zoning requirements (e.g., height, setback or density).	Subordinate authorities: Planning, Zoning or Zoning Appeals Board or Hearing Examiner. (Appeals to council may be permitted.)	Yes. A second public hearing required if board's decision is appealed to council.	Zoning restrictions create hardship for landowner and prevent reasonable use of land.	Easier than rezoning, but varies with current government policies in area.
C. Conditional Use (Special Exception)	Use is lawful if approved by public agency or local council.	Usually subordinate public agencies—sometimes town or county council.	Yes.	At discretion of specified board.	Depending on use, may be easier or harder than getting a variance approved.

NOTE: It is imperative that local, county, and state zoning regulations and ordinances be thoroughly checked for each situation. The above table is for reference only. Check with your local zoning board.

Appendix II

Business Opportunities, General Resources, and References

Accounting	*Essentials of Accounting,* Robert N. Anthony. Addison-Wesley, 1983.
Advertising	*Handbook of Small Business Advertising,* Michael J. Anthony. Addison-Wesley, 1981.
Business Periodicals	*Ayer Directory of Publications.* IMS Press, Annual. *Business Periodicals Index.* H. W. Wilson, Monthly, Quarterly, Annual.
Economic Conditions	*Business Statistics.* Government Printing Office, Biannual. *Economic Report of the President,* President of the United States. Government Printing Office, Annual.
Franchising	*Own Your Own Franchise,* Ray Bard and Sheila Henderson. Addison-Wesley, 1987. *The Complete Handbook of Franchising,* David D. Seltz. Addison-Wesley, 1982. *Directory of Franchising Organizations.* Pilot Books, Annual.
Labor	*Employment and Earnings. State and Areas, Based on the Standard Industrial Classification.* Government Printing Office, Annual. Handbook of Labor Statistics. Government Printing Office, Biennial.
Management	*Strategic Management Skills,* Daniel J. Power, et al. Addison-Wesley, 1986. *Managing Operations in Emerging Companies,* Clifford A. Morton. Addison-Wesley, 1984.
Marketing	*Marketing in Emerging Companies,* Robert T. Davis, et al. Addison-Wesley, 1984. *Handbook of Retail Promotion Ideas,* Reuben Guberman. Addison-Wesley, 1981. *Handbook of Innovative Marketing Techniques,* David D. Seltz. Addison-Wesley, 1981.
Small Business	*Small Business Financing,* Shepard's et al. McGraw-Hill, 1983. *Small Business Sourcebook.* Gale Research, 1982.

OTHER RESOURCES AND REFERENCES

Business   *American Management Association.* 135 W. 50th Street,
Associations   N.Y., NY 10020.

Business Seminars   *"How to Buy and Sell Business Opportunities"* and
                        "Business Opportunity Appraiser." By American
                        Business Consultants, Inc., 1540 Nuthatch Lane,
                        Sunnyvale, CA 94087 (Telephone: 408-732-8931
                        and 408-738-3011).

Business Forms   American Business Consultants, Inc., 1540 Nuthatch
and Cassettes   Lane, Sunnyvale, CA 94087 (Telephone: 408-732-
                        8931 and 408-738-3011).

Consumer   *Consumer Information Catalog.* Free.
Information
Center—Pueblo,
CO 81009

Small Business   Washington, D.C. 20416.
Administration   Each of the 75 local offices of the SBA (call 800-368-
                        5855 for the one nearest you) offers a list of
                        courses and SBA publications. The SBA also
                        offers counseling through SCORE (Service Corps
                        of Retired Executives).

Superintendent of   Washington, D.C. 20402
Documents—   *Consumer's Guide to Federal Publications.* Free.
United States   *Government Periodicals and Subscription Services.* Free.
Government   *Ratio Analysis for Small Business.* Management Series
Printing Office   20.
                        Subject Bibliography. SB-004. Free.